Stay Healthy with G6PD Deficiency

Dale R. Baker

Author and Creator of G6PDDeficiency.org

Dale R. Baker is the creator and operator of the website G6PDDeficiency.org. He also has a severe form of G6PD Deficiency associated with chronic hemolytic anemia. He is dedicated to helping those with this enzymopathy learn to live healthier lives and avoid the complications associated with it, as well as promote greater awareness and knowledge among professional health care personnel. He loves cooking and has spent the past several years researching what foods are best for staying healthy with G6PD Deficiency and answering questions about what to and not to eat on the forum at g6pddeficiency.org.

Dale lives in the foothills of the Sierra Mountains in California with his adorable wife, Melody, and their two pets Red and Jake.

Staying Healthy

Recipes & Health Tips for People with G6PD Deficiency

A Valuable Reference Guide for Eating Safely!

Dale.Baker@g6pddeficiency.org

Published by: G6PDD PUBLISHING

Published by G6PDD PUBLISHING
Visit us at:
g6pddeficiency.org

Author: Dale R. Baker
Layout and Design by Melody W. Baker
ISBN-13: 978-0-9861768-0-7Melody W. Baker

ISBN-13: 978-0-9861768-0-7

IMPORTANT:
The information in this book reflects the author's experiences and opinions and is not intended to replace medical advice.

Before beginning this or any other nutritional regimen, consult with a physician to be sure it is appropriate for you.

Contents

Acknowledgments:

I am grateful for the input and encouragement of the hundreds of people who belong to the forum at g6pddeficiency.org.
Especially medical professionals like
Dr. Dorothy Ogundu,
who tirelessly dedicate their time and resources toward the understanding and treatment of G6PD Deficiency.

I am also grateful to the people on the forum who faithfully respond to countless inquiries and comments from parents, medical professionals, and other individuals who so desperately need their questions answered about how to deal with, and treat, the symptoms of G6PD Deficiency.

A very special thanks goes to my wife,
Melody W. Baker,
who has helped make this book possible. Her encouragement and help with writing, designing and editing has been monumental. Without her, this book may never have been written.

Introduction

The first question that should be answered is: "What on earth is G6PD Deficiency?"

It seems odd to me that 10% of the world's population (600 million people) would suffer from an enzymopathy, and yet few have ever heard of it. Basically, G6PD Deficiency is a genetic disorder of the X chromosome which causes the body to produce less than normal amounts of Glucose-6-Phosphate Dehydrogenaze (G6PD). Among other things, this enzyme regulates the production of reduced glutathione, which is the body's big gun antioxidant. This leaves red blood cells (RBCs) susceptible to damage from oxidative stress.

When certain foods, drugs and other substances that cause oxidative stress are ingested, or otherwise enter the body, they cause damage to red blood cells. Damaged RBCs then die and can clog up the very fine blood vessels in the eye, causing eye problems; bilirubin is also released into the blood stream, accumulates in the skin and brain which in turn causes the skin to turn a yellowish color and if concentrations are high enough, it can cause brain damage. If more RBCs die than the body can replace (hemolysis), the number of RBCs available to carry oxygen to the body is reduced. Depending on the severity of the hemolysis, the patient may need to be hospitalized for a blood transfusion. If the hemolysis cannot be stopped, and blood is not received soon enough, death can occur.

One researcher made the comment that we with G6PD Deficiency are the canaries in the coal mine. What is bad for us is bad for others, our systems are just more fragile. Oxidative stress causes many problems, including some forms of cancer, so learning to avoid it, is good for everyone.

The purpose of this book is to teach people and their families with this disorder how to maintain a healthy body through eating foods that are not only safe, but are rich in a variety of nutrients. Although the dietary suggestions throughout this book are vital for good health for people with G6PDD, others may find that the dietary information will serve as a guide for healthy eating. If you wish to understand more about this disorder, please see http://g6pddeficiency.org.

–Dale R. Baker
Author & person with G6PDD

Vitamins cannot be made in the body, so they have to be provided by the food we eat.

–Fitnesshealthzone.com

CHAPTER 1

Vitamins & Antioxidants

At first glance, you may be curious why some of the ingredients are highlighted in red. It is because they either contain substantial amounts of the *B vitamins* which are essential for the formation of new red blood cells, or they contain high amounts of *antioxidants* which are known to reduce oxidative stress.

Vitamin B_2 *(or riboflavin)* is important for body growth, reproduction and red cell production. It also helps the body release energy from carbohydrates. Dairy products, leafy green vegetables, nuts, fruits, organ meats and fish are excellent sources.

Vitamin B_6 assists the body in creating antibodies in the immune system. It helps the body maintain normal nerve function and is needed for the formation of hemoglobin within the red blood cells. It also helps increase the amount of oxygen carried by hemoglobin. The higher the protein intake, the more need there is for vitamin B_6, as it is needed to process proteins in the body. Potatoes, bananas, chicken breasts, and pork are the highest in vitamin B_6.

Vitamin B_9 *(Folate and folic acid)* Folate occurs naturally in fresh foods, whereas folic acid is the synthetic form found in supplements. Your body needs folate to produce red blood cells, as well as components of the nervous system. It is used to treat megeloblastic anemia, which is caused by deficiency in folate and vitamin B_{12}. Folic acid also helps in the formation and creation of DNA and maintaining normal brain function. It is vital for proper cell growth and development of the embryo. Organ meats, beef jerky, green-leafy vegetables and sunflower seeds are good sources of vitamin B_9, however, it can be easily destroyed by overcooking.

Vitamin B_{12} is important for metabolism. It helps in the formation of red blood cells and in the maintenance of the central nervous system. Vitamin B_{12} is the one vitamin that is available *only* from *fish, poultry, meat* or dairy sources in food.

Vitamin C is one of the most important of all vitamins. It protects our body's tissue from the damage of oxidation. Free radicals, which are potentially damaging by-products of the body's metabolism, can cause cell damage that may contribute to the development of cardiovascular disease and cancer. Vitamin C has also been found by scientists to be an effective antiviral agent.

Ascorbic acid, a synthetic form of vitamin C, is on the contraindicated list, and it is added to many prepared foods. Manufacturers make no distinction on their food labels between natural vitamin C and ascorbic ccid. To my knowledge, the natural variety found in fruits and vegetables does not cause a problem for those with G6PDD.

Vitamins A, D, E, & K are in fat. Reduced fat milk for example has to be fortified with vitamin D, while whole milk does not. We do not recommend diets high in fat; however, we do suggest a diet with a reasonable amount so that these vitamins can be obtained naturally. If you are concerned about your cholesterol levels the July 2009 issue of the Harvard Health Letter suggests that saturated and trans fats have a much bigger affect on blood cholesterol levels. In *Chapter 2: Converting Recipes*, is a list of acceptable fats, and ways to use them in your cooking.

Conclusion:

Adding ingredients that are rich in vitamins and nutrients will provide much needed antioxidants, as well as the building blocks the body needs to create new red blood cells. For example, nutrient rich spinach or mild squash can be added to eggs, meatloaf, soups, while affecting the taste very little. You can chop these, and other vegetables so small that they look like an herb so people don't suspect you are feeding them a healthier diet. (We even add a little to our smoothies.) Great for getting around picky eaters. For more ideas about making your favorite dishes, healthier, see: *Chapter 3: Feeding Infants and Children.*

For more information about these vitamins,
as well as other vitamins and antioxidants, go to:
http://www.healthalternatives2000.com/vitamins-nutrition-chart.html.
Much of the information, as well as the lists of nutrient rich foods
in this book, are from this website.

The following foods are also known to be excellent sources of B vitamins, as well as vitamins A, D, E, and K. You will find these food items listed in *red* in the recipe ingredients, and in the index.

Seeds and Nuts:

barley
buckwheat
rye
spelt
chestnuts
filberts/Hazelnuts
oats
quinoa
sunflower Seeds
wheat

Proteins:

beef
cheddar cheese
chicken
eggs
caviar
herring
liver
salmon
sardines
tuna
goat cheese
lamb
pork
turkey breast
veal
yogurt
sour cream
duck

Fruits and Vegetables

Planning meals using fruits and vegetables that are in season will ensure that you and your family are getting the most nutrients and taste possible for your food dollar, as many of the antioxidant vitamins are lost when produce is frozen or canned. A diet rich in fruits and vegetables is necessary for optimum health.

Fruits and Vegetables:

artichokes (spring)
asparagus (spring)
berries (summer)
broccoli (winter, spring)
cabbage (spring)
corn (summer)
cranberries (fall)
grapefruit (winter)
grapes (fall)
mangos (spring)
mushrooms (fall)
okra (summer)
oranges (fall, winter)
papayas (winter)
peppers, raw (summer)
pineapple (spring)
pomegranates (fall)
potatoes (fall, winter)
pumpkin (fall)
spinach (spring, fall, winter)
summer squash (summer, fall)
sweet potatoes (fall)
winter squash (winter, spring)
watermelons (summer)

Consumers who wish to safeguard health understand the role of a healthy diet. A healthy diet choice is possible only when we read the food labels and decipher it's nutritional content.

- targetwoman.com

CHAPTER 2

Converting Recipes

Use common sense when converting recipes and don't assume that a small amount of something contraindicated will be okay. Depending on the person, sometimes a very small amount will cause a hemolytic crises.

How to Make Recipes Safe

Most recipes can easily be made safe for G6PD Deficient people, but making them more nutritious is just as important. This can be done in three ways:

- **Removing harmful ingredients**
- **Substituting more healthy ingredients**
- **Adding nutrient rich ingredients.**

For example: If a recipe calls for margarine, use butter, coconut oil, olive oil or palm oil instead. You can leave out the beans or peanuts in most recipes, or replace them with other nutritious vegetables.

Contraindicated Foods and Additives

It is almost impossible to list every food and additive known to be contraindicated, especially when many of the additives have multiple names, or are made from substances or chemicals that are contradinicated. (Hence, the reason for this cookbook.) However, we have added the most common contraindicated foods and additives to watch out for. Just remember: "If in doubt... cook without."

Artificial Food Color

Many products manufactured today in the United States (including many drugs), are "enhanced" with artificial food colors. This is not a good thing for people with G6PD Deficiency. Blue food color has been known to cause hemolysis in many people. A safer way to go is to just avoid all artificial food colors, as some are made by mixing blue with other colors.

Recipes which call for flavored gelatin or Kool-aid are difficult to convert and require some creative thinking. Some manufacturers put food color in fruit products without saying so on the label. They get by with it because they put in only small amounts of food coloring, but even small amounts have been known to cause a hemolytic crisis.

In the last few years, many companies have started using natural agents such as Betanin, turmeric, saffron, paprika and elderberry as dyes, which are much safer.

Prepared Foods

This is the hardest category to find substitutes for. Canned goods, bread, filled pasta, deli items, etc., can all contain harmful products. It is important to read all labels to check for contraindicated things before using them in meal preparation. However, most recipes that call for prepared foods do so as a matter of convenience. Most can be made from scratch, and either be used immediately, or preserved for later use. One common item is cream of mushroom or cream of chicken soup. Recipes for these soup bases can be found in the soup chapter. Also, a good organic chicken stock or a product called "Better Than Bouillon" can be used as a substitute for both bouillon and for chicken soup.

Wine

Wine has two problems. One, it usually contains sulfites (especially red wine) and it contains alcohol (or ethanol). Both substances can cause hemolysis.

Food Preservatives (Sulfites, Ascorbic Acid)

Due to the time it takes for food to get from the source to your table, many items contain food preservatives such as sulfites or ascorbic acid. These substances have been declared safe by the FDA, but they are not safe for individuals with G6PDD as they can cause hemolysis.

The best choice whenever possible is organic products because they are not suppose to contain preservatives. Always check the package before buying them.

Sulfites (not sulfAtes) are used extensively as a preservative and have been reported to cause hemolysis by many people. They can be found in some dried fruits and veggies, processed meats, wine, vinegar and many other places, so look at labels carefully. Sulfites also cannot be metabolized by those with G6PDD. Do not confuse *sulfites* with *sulfur,* which is required for good health, and can be obtained safely from onions and garlic.

Bitter Gourd & Bitter Melon

These are plants grown in India, Southeast Asia, China, Africa and the Caribbean and have culinary uses in stir-fries, soup, tea, prepared with potatoes, curry and other things. They cause hemolysis in some G6PDD people.

Menthol

Mint obtained from mint leaves does not cause hemolysis, but the synthetic version (menthol) does and should be avoided. If the label says menthol, it is most likely the synthetic version. If the label says mint oil, or peppermint oil, it is obtained from the mint or peppermint plant, and is safe.

Mayonnaise, Salad Dressing, and other Fats

I have not had much luck finding mayonnaise that is not made from soy oil, but you may be able to find it at a health food store, or you can make your own quite easily. (See the recipe in *Chapter 5: Sandwiches & Salads.*) Sour cream or plain yogurt can also be used as a substitute in some recipes. One the most versatile "healthy" oils for cooking is extra virgin coconut oil. It has a better taste, and smells just a little like coconuts.

There are different grades and types of fats and oils. Unfortunately, the most common fats are often the worst. The oil is extracted from plants by several methods. Cold press, which produces the best oil, can be a bit more expensive. Another method extracts oil by using chemicals such as hexane to get more of the fat from the plant and reduce costs. Trace amounts of these solvents are still in the oil. *Cold pressed oil should be used whenever possible, as it is free of hexane.*

Fats should not be heated above their smoke point as it causes changes in the oil's chemical makeup, which can cause the oil to become carcinogenic. When choosing what kind of fat to use, pick one that won't smoke at the temperatures called for in the recipe. A list of safe oils, fats and their uses can be found at the end of this chapter.

Legumes

Legumes are plants from the *Leguminosae* family. Basically, they are plants that have seed pods that, when ripe, split along both sides. Legumes will probably be the hardest ingredient to substitute because they are widely used for so many things.

Many people with G6PDD have a condition called "Favism", which means that fava beans will cause serious hemolysis. For these people, other legumes can be a problem as well.

The list of legumes, and products made from them, is very large and each region of the world seems to have a favorite legume that is used as a staple food. Fava beans (also called broad beans) are considered a staple in Egypt and Iran. The most common legumes eaten in the United States are green beans, dried beans, peas, peanuts, soy, and lentils.

When I first began avoiding legumes, I left the grocery store many times without buying anything because I could not find products I needed which did not contain soy and/ or peanut oil. (Both soy and peanuts are listed as two of the top ten allergens in the world, so it is amazing that they are used in so many products.) I have since had success substituting rice, barley, or other grains for legumes. A mix of grains can be a very healthy alternative.

The chart on the following pages lists the most common legumes that are used around the world. For the most up-to-date list, please visit g6pddeficiency.org.

Legumes

Although fava or broad beans are the main cause of hemolysis among the legumes, many others can also cause low level hemolysis. For an up-to-date list visit: g6pddeficiency.org/index.php?cmd=legumes.

Beans

* aduki bean
* adzuki bean
* anasazi beans
* appaloosa bean
* asuki bean
* azufrado bean
* azuki bean
* baby lima bean
* bayo bean
* bengal bean
* black azuki bean
* black bean
* black turtle bean
* bolita bean
* bonavist bean
* borlotti bean
* Boston bean
* Boston navy bean
* broad bean
* brown speckled cow bean
* buffalo bean
* butter bean
* butterscotch calypso bean
* calypso bean
* canaria bean
* canario bean
* cannellini bean
* chestnut lima bean
* chili bean
* Christmas lima bean
* cabeca-de-frade
* chiporro
* coco bean
* coco blanc bean
* crab eye bean

* Couhage
* Cowage
* Cowhage
* Cowitch
* cranberry bean
* dermason bean
* Dolichos pruriens
* edamame
* Egyptian bean
* Egyptian white broad bean
* English bean
* European soldier bean
* eye of the goat bean
* faba
* fagiolo romano
* fava bean
* fava-coceira
* fayot
* fazolia bean
* feijao bean
* feve
* field pea
* flageolet
* fool
* foul
* frijo bola roja
* frijole negro
* Fuji mame
* ful
* great Northern bean
* green gram
* haba
* habas
* haricot blanc bean
* horse bean
* hyacinth bean
* itchy bean
* Indian bean

List of Legumes (continued)

* Jackson wonder bean
* Jacob's cattle bean
* krame
* kidney bean
* lablab bean
* lima bean
* lingot bean
* lupini bean
* Madagascar bean
* maicoba bean
* maine Yellow eye
* mayocoba bean
* marrow bean
* mauritius bean
* Mexican black bean
* Mexican red bean
* molasses face bean
* mortgage lifter bean
* mortgage runner bean
* moth dal
* mucuna bean
* mucuna pruriens
* mucuna prurita
* mung bean
* mung pea
* mungo bean
* navy bean
* nescafé
* orca bean
* pea bean
* pearl haricot
* Peruano bean
* Peruvian bean
* picapica
* pink bean
* pinto bean
* pó de mico
* prince bean
* purple appaloosa bean
* rajma
* rattlesnake bean
* red ball bean
* red bean
* red eye bean
* red chori
* red kidney bean
* red Oriental bean
* rice bean
* rosecoco bean
* roman bean
* runner bean
* saluggia
* salugia bean
* scarlet runner bean
* Setae Siliquae Hirsutae
* shell bean
* small red bean
* small white bean
* soy bean
* soya bean
* soybean
* Spanish black bean
* Spanish Tolosana bean
* speckled brown cow bean
* Steuben yellow bean
* Steuben yellow eye bean
* Stizolobium pruriens
* Sweet bean
* Swedish brown bean
* tapary bean
* tepary bean
* Tiensin red bean
* Tolosana bean
* tongues of fire bean
* tremmocos
* trout bean
* turtle bean
* turtle soup bean
* vallarta bean
* val
* velvet bean
* wax bean
* whit bean
* white kidney bean
* white pea bean
* Windsor bean
* Yankee bean
* yellow Indian woman bean
* yin yang bean

Snap Beans

* asparagus bean
* asparagus pea
* bodi
* boonchi
* chepil
* Chinese long bean
* dau gok
* dow gok
* dragon tongue bean
* French bean
* French green bean
* four-angled bean
* goa verts
* Italian flat bean

List of Legumes (continued)

* long bean
* manila bean
* princess pea
* romano bean
* runner bean
* sator
* snap bean
* string bean
* Thailand long bean
* wax bean
* winged bean
* winged pea
* yard-long bean

Bean Products

* black beans in salted sauce
* black salted fermented bean
* Chinese black bean
* dow see
* fermented black bean
* frijoles refritos
* refried beans
* salted black bean
* salty black bean

Edible Pods

* Chinese pea pod
* Chinese pea
* Chinese snow pea
* edible-podded pea
* mange-tout pea
* snow pea
* sugar pea
* sugar snap

Lentils

* arhar
* arhar dal
* beluga black lentil
* beluga lentil
* Bengal gram
* black beluga lentil
* black chickpeas
* black gram
* black lentil
* brown lentil
* channa dal
* chana dal
* chilke urad
* chowli dal
* continental lentil
* dal
* daal
* dhaal
* dhal
* dhall
* Egyptian lentil
* French green lentils
* German lentil
* gram dal
* green lentil
* horse gram
* Indian brown lentil
* kala channa
* kali dal
* lablab beans
* lentilles du Puy
* lentilles vertes du

Peas

* Bengal gram
* black-eyed pea
* black-eye bean
* black-eye pea
* black-eyed suzy
* ceci bean
* cici bean
* China bean
* chawli
* chickpea
* chick-pea
* chole
* congo pea
* congo bean
* cowpea
* crowder pea
* dried peas
* Egyptian pea
* field peas
* fresh peas
* gandules
* garbanzo bean
* garbanzo pea
* garbonzo bean
* goongoo pea
* green pea
* green matar dal
* green split pea
* gunga pea
* gungo pea
* kabuli channa
* kabli chana
* kabli channa

* lobhia
* lombia
* no-eyed peas
* pigeon pea
* pois chiches
* poor man's pea
* Southern pea
* white chickpea
* yellow pea
* yellow matar dal
* yellow-eyed pea

Puy

* masar
* masar dal
* masoor
* masoor dal
* matki
* moath
* moong dal
* mussoor
* mussoor dal
* petite beluga lentil
* Puy lentil
* red lentil
* toor
* toor dal
* tuvar
* tuvar dal
* tur
* tur dal
* urad dal
* val dal
* white lentil
* yellow lentil

Soy Products

* abura-age
* aburage
* aka miso
* akamiso
* atsu-age
* atsuage
* bamboo yuba
* barley miso
* awase miso
* firm tofu
* foo yu
* fried bean curd
* fu jook pei
* fu yi
* fu yu
* genmai miso
* hat-cho miso
* hatcho miso
* inaka miso
* inariage
* kinu-goshi
* kirazu
* kyoto shiro miso
* mame miso
* mamemiso
* medium tofu
* mellow white miso
* miso
* mugi miso
* nama-age
* nama nori san
* nato
* natto
* nattou
* nigari tofu
* okara
* plant protein
* preserved bean curd
* pressed tofu
* protein crumbles
* red miso
* regular tofu
* roasted soybeans
* sendai miso
* shinshu miso
* shiro miso
* shiromiso
* silken tofu
* soft tofu
* soy cheese
* soy mayonnaise
* soy milk
* soy milk skins
* soy sour cream
* soy nuts
* soy yogurt
* soya cheese
* soya mayonnaise
* soybean curd
* soybean paper
* soybean paste
* soynuts
* soynut butter
* sui-doufu
* sweet miso
* sweet white miso
* tempe

List of Legumes (continued)

* tempeh
* texturized soy protein
* texturized vegetable protein
* tofu
* tofu mayonnaise
* tofu sour cream
* TSP
* TVP
* uba
* unohana
* usuage
* vegetable protein
* wet bean curd
* white miso
* yellow miso
* yuba

Vegetable Gum Thickeners

(These are either made from legumes, or can be made from legumes)

* albumin - from peas
* acacia gum
* carob bean gum
* flavoring or natural flavoring
* gum arabic
* guar gum
* lecithin
* monosodium glutamate (from soy)
* tara seed gum
* tragacanth
* vegetable broth (soy or even fava beans)
* vegetable emulsifier
* vegetable glycerin
* vegetable gelatin
* vegetable stabilizer

Other Legumes

* alfalfa sprouts
* astragalus (herbal medicine)
* carob (chocolate substitute)
* fenugreek
* jicama
* licorice
* senna or cassia
* singkamas
* tamarind
* vetch family (not normally used for food)

Other Foods Likely to Contain Hidden Soy or Legume Additives

* artificial butter flavor
* baked goods
* candies
* canned meats or tuna
* canned soups
* chips
* Chinese food
* gravy mixes
* infant formula
* low-fat cheeses or cheese substitutes
* margarine
* sausages, hot dogs, processed meats
* sauces (Worcestershire. sweet and sour etc.)
* salad dressings
* stock or bouillon
* tofutti
* powdered foods

Facts about Cooking with Oils

Fats or Oils	Cooking Uses	Smoke Point °F	Smoke Point °C
Almond Oil	Used in sauté and stir fry of Oriental foods.	420°F	216°C
Avocado Oil	Stir frying, searing	520°F	271°C
Butter	Baking, cooking	350°F	177°C
Clarified Butter	Frying, sautéing	375-485°F (depending on purity)	190-250°C (depending on purity)
Coconut Oil	coatings, confectionary, shortening	350°F	177°C
Corn Oil	Frying, salad dressings, shortening	450°F	232°C
Grapeseed Oil	Excellent choice of cooking oil for sautéing or frying. Also used in salad dressings.	392°F	200°C
Hazelnut Oil	Salad dressings, marinades and baked goods.	430°F	221°C
Lard	Baking and frying	370°F	182 °C
Macadamia Nut Oil	Sauté, pan fry, sear, deep fry, stir fry, grill, broil, baking.	390°F	199 °C
Olive Oil	cooking, salad dressings, sauté, pan fry, sear, deep fry, stir fry, grill, broil, baking	Extra Virgin - 320°F Virgin - 420°F Pomace - 460°F Extra Light - 468°F	160°C 216°C 238°C 242°C
Palm Oil	Cooking, flavoring	446°F	230°C
Rice Bran Oil	Frying, sauté, salad dressings, baking, dipping oils	490°F	254°C
Safflower Oil	Margarine, mayonnaise, salad dressings	450°F	232°C
Sesame Oil	Cooking, salad dressings	410°F	232°C
Sunflower Oil	Cooking, margarine, salad dressings, shortening	450°F	232°C
Walnut Oil	Sauté, pan fry, sear, deep fry, stir fry, grill, broil	400°F	204°C

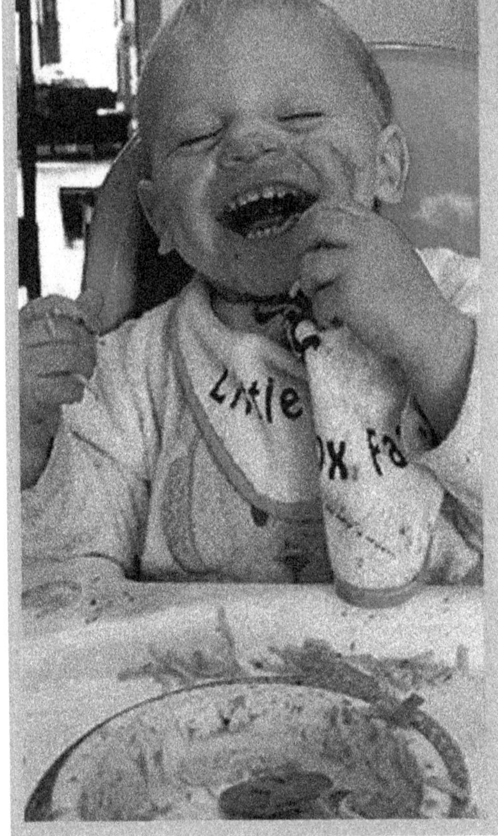

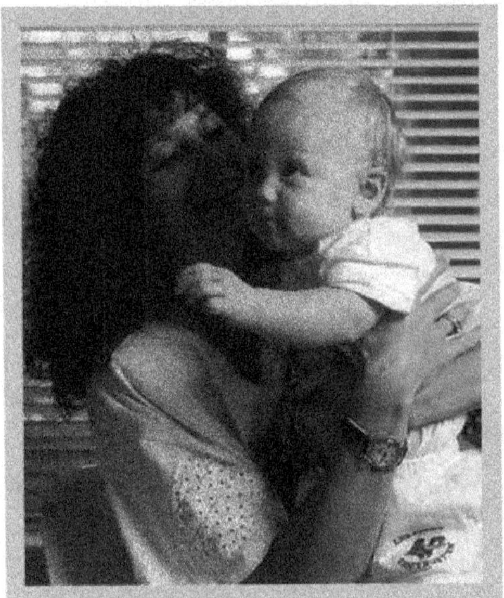

CHAPTER 3

Feeding Babies & Children

Getting your children to eat nutritious food can be a challenge, but it can be done if you use the right persuasion.

First and foremost: DO NOT tell them the food you want them to eat is nutritious. They will throw a fit and their eyes will glaze over when you try to explain. At least that has been my experience in raising three boys.

Second: DO NOT let them see the veggies and nutritious stuff you lovingly put into their food. The gag reflex will take over and they won't touch it.

Third: Avoid food fights. If your children get into the habit of fighting over what food they are going to eat, you will fight that battle forever. Ease them into healthy foods. Many nutritionists say that a child has to see a new food four or five times before they will try it. Just set a good example and keep offering them healthy foods.

Another trick is to get your children involved in cooking and/or growing food. It is surprising to see how pride can change a child's taste buds.

Essential equipment includes a blender, or other device, for reducing food to a paste consistency. The idea for infants is to feed them the same food you eat, only processed in a blender. For older children, the blender will reduce food they don't like to a form that can be hidden in other foods. Just remember to start out small and add more as they get used to the taste.

Make your children's food as colorful and fun as possible–and don't expect them to jump on board right from the start.

Fix smoothies. Add the good stuff in small amounts first, then make sure they see you add a scoop of ice cream or some other favorite food.

If they like meat loaf or pizza, just add a small amount of very finely chopped spinach to the sauce or under the other toppings so it won't be noticed. After a while they will get used to the taste and maybe even like it.

Children love peanut butter and a great substitute ingredient is almond butter or another of the tree nut butters. These have become much more available in the past few years. Just substitute another tree nut butter for peanut butter in any of your children's favorite recipes or sandwiches.

Feeding your infant

If at all possible breast feed your baby. Infant formulas are very high in sugar (it's listed in the ingredients but broken up into several types so it isn't first), they all have contraindicated substances in them (like soy and ascorbic acid as well as other artificial ingredients–like vitamins). But if breast feeding is simply not possible, goat's milk or whole cow's milk should be used.

Most doctors recommend the transition to solid food start at about six months or so. Rice cereal is fine, but do get your child onto the food you eat as soon as your doctor recommends. Don't be afraid to fix their food yourself instead of buying it from the store. They will be much better off and the food will be better as well.

If young children get used to eating what you eat early enough, the transition will be a lot easier. As soon as possible, find your baby's favorite food and start putting small amounts of greens, liver, fruits and veggies into it and start getting your child used to these foods if they won't eat them by themselves.

Supplements

Most supplements are derived from artificial sources and studies are now saying that multiple vitamins just do not do what we have been told they do. Please supplement cautiously when necessary and not at all when your baby is healthy and eating good foods.

One last remark: Peer pressure can be daunting, or, it can be used to your advantage. Be creative!

In summary, I would recommend the following suggestions:

1. If you can't breast feed, use goat's milk or whole cow's milk

2. Feed your child what you eat as soon as possible. If possible, the whole family should avoid contraindicated foods and eat right. That way your child won't feel left out or "different."

3. Supplement with vitamins only as necessary and even then, be cautious.

4. Make sure that your family, friends, school, church, etc., know to not feed your child unless they get permission from you.

5. Teach your child about G6PDD and how important it is to stay away from contraindicated substances. Don't make it a big secret or something awful. It isn't. Everyone has problems. Some children are allergic to things, or have diabetes, or cancer, or whatever. There are a lot of things worse than having to avoid a few substances and eat right.

Go to: *http://g6pddeficiency.org/index.php?cmd=contraindicated* for the latest list of things to avoid.

Recipes for Children

Recipes for children are scattered throughout the book. The list below are recipes that traditionally are favorites of most children. They are generally more mildly seasoned, and the veggies are cleverly disguised.

Eating a healthy, protein rich breakfast keeps you going all day long without feeling hungry again an hour later.

- Dale Baker

CHAPTER 4

Breakfast

It's important that the first meal of the day be rich in antioxidants and contain a complete protein as well.

Avoid cereals that contain legumes (beans, peas, peanuts, etc.) and fruit drinks that contain artificial food coloring (especially blue), sulfites and other contraindicated substances. Ascorbic acid is also a common additive to prepared foods and should be avoided. (For a complete list of contraindicated foods please visit our website: g6pddeficiency.org, which is updated regularly.)

A basic grain mix is made using approximately 50% wheat and 10% each of other grains. For example:

6 cups wheat
1 cup barley
1 cup rye
1 cup brown rice
1 cup oat groats

Virtually any combination of the following grains is beneficial, depending on the taste preferences of your family. The health benefits are from the website: www.grainmix.com, who is a distributor of different types of grain mixes, all from organic sources. The following mix is called Grainmix 9:

AMARANTH – completes wheat protein
BUCKWHEAT – helps circulation
OATS – lowers cholesterol
BROWN RICE – promotes growth
WHEAT – decrease cancer risk
BARLEY – less asthma
MILLET – soothes digestion
QUINOA – stops migraine
RYE – appetite suppressant

NOTE: Before ordering from grainmix.com, or other suppliers, make sure you tell them you have G6PD Deficiency, and that you cannot eat legumes.

DO NOT SUBSTITUTE MARGARINE FOR BUTTER!

Multigrain Buttermilk Pancakes

Contributed by Melody W. Baker

1		*egg*
1 1/4	*cups*	*buttermilk or sour milk*
1/2	*tsp*	*baking soda*
1 1/4	*cup*	*multigrain flour**
1	*tsp*	*sugar*
2	*Tbsp*	*butter or virgin coconut oil*
1	*tsp*	*baking powder*
1/2	*tsp*	*salt*

1. Heat griddle slowly while mixing batter.
2. Beat egg well with a fork or whisk.
3. Beat in milk and baking soda.
4. Beat in remaining ingredients.

*Note: See the beginning of the chapter for a discussion on multigrain mixes and their nutritional value.

Stove-top Breakfast with Antioxidants

1/4	*lb*	*sulfite-free bacon, sausage, beef or chicken (ground or cubed)*
3	*Tbsp*	*diced onion*
3	*Tbsp*	*diced bell pepper (may substitute part or all with hot peppers)*
4		*eggs*
1	*dollop*	*sour cream (use Daisy brand, or one that is free of non-milk ingredients)*
2	*Tbsp*	*tomato (diced)*
1	*cup*	*potatoes (cubed or shredded)*
2	*Tbsp*	*butter or virgin coconut oil*
1	*tsp*	*oregano (dried), (or 1 Tbsp fresh)*
1/2	*cup*	*cheese (grated)*

1. Add butter to large hot skillet then add potatoes. Cook for 2 minutes on medium heat.

2. Add meat and continue to cook until potatoes just start to brown.

3. Add onion, bell pepper, oregano, salt and pepper.

4. Crack eggs into a small bowl and beat well.

5. Add sour cream and tomatoes and mix well.

Add egg mixture to potatoes and sprinkle cheese on top. Cover and cook on medium low until set (about 5 minutes).

Serves four.

Variation: For a great way to add greens to your family's diet, add spinach or other greens to the pan just before adding the egg mixture.

Breakfast Sandwich

4		*multigrain muffins, or flat bread*
8		*eggs*
1/2	*cup*	*shredded cheese or four slices of cheese*
1		*ripe tomato*
2-3	*cups*	*spinach (rinsed)*
		salt and pepper
	pinch	*oregano, thyme or other favorite herb*
2	*Tbsp*	*butter or olive oil*

1. If using muffins, split and toast; or warm flat bread.

2. Cook spinach by bringing approximately 1/2 cup water to a boil in a large skillet with a tight-fitting lid. Add spinach and cook covered for about 5 minutes. Remove and allow to drain in a colander.

3. Beat the eggs in a small bowl with a whisk or fork until light yellow. Add a tablespoon of your favorite salsa or sour cream for additional flavor. Make four omelets to fit on the muffins. Set aside.

4. To assemble, put some cheese on the bottom muffin and then top with 1/4 of the spinach, an omelet, slice of tomato and more cheese.

Multigrain Cooked Cereal

Contributed by Rebecca Berg

6	*cups*	*wheat*
1	*cup*	*amaranth*
1	*cup*	*buckwheat*
1	*cup*	*oats*
1	*cup*	*brown rice*
1	*cup*	*barley*
1	*cup*	*millet*
1	*cup*	*quinoa*

1. Mix together all ingredients. Grind as needed for cereal, flour, etc.

2. Cook in the microwave or stove top as you would any hot cereal.

Studies show that flour or cereals that are ground fresh have more nutrients, as once the grain is broken, just like fruits, they start to oxidize. Freezing flour and cereals made from whole grains also help to slow down the oxidation process.

Mixing grains together makes breads and cereals much lighter in texture, and also much healthier. If your family is not used to whole grains, start by substiuting half the white flour with freshly ground flour in your muffins, biscuits, etc. Gradually adding more as your family gets used to the flavor and texture. The flour has a nice nutty taste, that most people really enjoy. Add raisins, chopped apples, or cinnamon as desired.

Helpful Tip: For baby's first cereal start with the brown rice, oatmeal and barley until their digestive system can handle the increased fiber. You can make a large batch and refridgerate it for about a week or so, then heat up servings up as needed.

Dutch Muesli

3	*cups*	*multigrain cereal mix (page 35)*
3	*cups*	*boiling water*
1/4	*cup*	*raw unsalted almonds (coarsely chopped)*
1/4	*cup*	*raisins*
1/4	*cup*	*dates (chopped)*
1/4	*cup*	*tart dried cherries*
1		*orange (juiced)*
1/4	*cup*	*honey*
1	*cup*	*plain yogurt*
1/2	*tsp*	*cinnamon*
1		*large apple (diced)*

1. Combine the grain and water in a glass bowl and allow to sit over night or until water is absorbed.

2. Mix remaining ingredients in another glass bowl.

3. Add wet grains to fruit mix and serve immediately. Keeps in the refrigerator for about four days.

Breakfast Cookies

3	cups	multigrain flour
2	tsp	baking powder
1/4	tsp	ground cloves
1/4	tsp	cinnamon
1/2	tsp	nutmeg
1/8	tsp	mace
1/8	tsp	cardamom
1/4	tsp	salt
1/2	cup	honey or agave nectar
1/2	cup	extra virgin olive oil, or virgin coconut oil
4		eggs
1/2	cup	blackstrap molasses (unsulfured)
1/2	cup	apple butter or apple sauce
1	Tbsp	vanilla
2	Tbsp	plain yogurt
1	cup	dried organic tart cherries or raisins
1	cup	almonds (chopped)
1/2	cup	dried cranberries

1. Preheat oven to 350°F (176°C). Prepare cookie sheets by lining with Silpat or parchment paper.

2. Stir all dry ingredients together in a large mixing bowl.

3. Cream olive oil and honey together until smooth

4. In a separate bowl, beat eggs together and then add to olive oil mixture. Mix well.

5. Add molasses, applesauce, vanilla and yogurt and mix well again.

6. Add cherries, cranberries and almonds. Mix well. You may have to use your own clean hands coated lightly with olive oil to mix properly. The dough should form a ball.

7. Wrap with plastic and refrigerate for an hour or two. Remove from refrigerator.

8. Using a soup spoon, make small balls with the batter and place on the cookie sheets and press down lightly with a fork.

9. Bake for 10 minutes or until lightly brown.

Country Sausage

1	*lb*	*ground pork*
1	*tsp*	*dried sage*
1	*tsp*	*dried thyme*
1	*tsp*	*salt*
1/4	*tsp*	*crushed red pepper*

1. Mix all the ingredients together and let sit in the refrigerator overnight to season through. Use as you would ground sausage purchased at the store.

Multigrain Muffins with Fruit

These muffins are full of antioxidants, whole grains and great goodness. Make them ahead and serve for breakfast when you just don't have time for anything else, or serve them with your favorite dish as a healthy addition.

1	cup	all-purpose flour
1	cup	multigrain flour
1	tsp	baking soda
1/2	tsp	salt
1/2	cup	butter, or virgin coconut oil
1	cup	sugar, or 3/4 cup agave
2		eggs
1	cup	fruit (dried, fresh or frozen)
1		orange (finely chopped, or put in blender)
		zest of one orange
8	ozs	yogurt (plain or flavored)

1. Preheat oven to 400°F (204°C) and butter a 12-cup muffin pan.
2. In large bowl, stir together flour, baking soda and salt.
3. In large mixer bowl cream butter and sugar. Add eggs and beat until fluffy.
4. Dice fruit into 1/4 inch or smaller pieces by hand or in a food processor fitted with the metal blade.
5. Stir fruit and orange zest into creamed butter mixture; stir in yogurt. Add fruit mixture all at once to dry ingredients and stir just until moistened.
6. Divide batter among prepared muffin cups. Bake in oven 15 to 17 minutes or until done.
7. Makes 12 muffins.

Note: This recipe can also be used to make 2 medium loaves of quick bread.

Multigrain Blueberry Pancakes

1/2	cup	*all-purpose flour*
1/2	cup	*multigrain flour*
1	tsp	*baking soda*
1/2	tsp	*salt*
1		*egg (slightly beaten)*
1	cup	*buttermilk*
2	Tbsp	*butter or virgin coconut oil*
1	cup	*fresh or frozen blueberries (rinsed, dried, and tossed in flour)*

1. Stir together flour, baking soda and salt in mixing bowl.

2. Beat eggs in separate bowl; stir in buttermilk and melted butter.

3. Add liquid mixture to dry ingredients, stirring just until blended. Fold in blueberries.

4. Heat greased griddle or skillet over medium heat or to 375°F (190°C). Griddle is ready when a few drops of water dropped on the griddle bubble and skitter rapidly around.

5. For each pancake, pour scant 1/4 cup batter onto hot griddle. Cook until puffed, bubbly and dry around edges. Turn and cook other side until golden brown.

6. This recipe yields about 9 (4-inch) pancakes.

Note: You can substitute most any fruit for the blueberries.

Fruit Pancake Sauce

3	*cups*	*fresh or frozen fruit*
4	*ozs*	*cottage cheese*
		sugar or agave to taste

1. Put all ingredients into a blender, and blend on medium until smooth.

Note: You can add other things like wheat germ, pomegranate juice concentrate, whey powder, etc., to make this sauce as healthy as possible.

Egg & Vegetable Casserole

2		*medium potatoes (diced 1/4")*
1	*cup*	*vegetables (diced)*
1/2	*cup*	*onions (diced)*
1/2	*cup*	*bell pepper (diced)*
1/2	*cup*	*spinach (cooked)*
1/2	*cup*	*ham (diced sulphite free)*
1/4	*cup*	*buttermilk or sour cream*
6		*eggs (well beaten)*
1	*cup*	*cheese (shredded)*
2	*Tbsp*	*butter or virgin coconut oil*
		salt & pepper to taste

1. Vegetables can be a mix of squash, eggplant, carrots, sweet potatoes turnips or any fleshy vegetable that is in season. Use your imagination.

2. Prepare potatoes and any other hard root vegetable, like carrots or sweet potatoes, and place in a hot pan with butter.

3. While the potatoes are cooking prepare the rest of the ingredients. Add the rest of the vegetables, onions, bell peppers and ham (may substitute your favorite breakfast meat) to the potatoes when they are beginning to soften and turn brown.

4. When vegetables are cooked, add the eggs mixed with the buttermilk. Cook until eggs are almost done. Stir a time or two.

5. Season with salt and pepper. You may add a few seasonings that your family likes at this point.

6. Add cheese and serve when eggs are done and cheese has melted.

Baked Eggs

eggs

cheese

mustard or curry sauce (optional)

salt & pepper to taste

1. Butter an oven-proof dish that is large enough to hold eggs and break eggs into it.

2. Cover eggs with cheese, mustard or curry sauce, etc.

3. Bake in a 350°F (176°C) oven for about 10 minutes.

4. Buttered bread crumbs may be placed on top before or after baking.

CHAPTER 5

Salads & Sandwiches

Salads should be a daily addition to your meals and may be either fruit, vegetable or a combination of the two.

The addition of fruit to a green salad makes a very nice enhancement. Choose any combination of fruits and vegetables depending on availability, except legumes, to make your salads more interesting.

Fruits and vegetables that are especially high in blood building vitamins or antioxidants are listed in red. Fresh oregano is one of the best antioxidants and can be added to your salads.

Avoid buying salad dressing at the store, if possible, as most store-bought dressings contain soy or other cheap oils. Salad dressings are easy to make yourself from a good quality olive oil and fresh ingredients. See the dressing recipes in this chapter.

Whenever possible buy or grow organic fruit and vegetables to avoid the chemicals used on commercial farms. Wash food thoroughly before using. If you are concerned about using raw eggs, please read the information in *Chapter 11: Beverages,* for ways to pasteurize your own eggs.

DO NOT SUBSTITUTE MARGARINE FOR BUTTER!

Fruit Salad

4	oz	yogurt
8	oz	heavy cream (whipped)
4		bananas (sliced)
2		apples (cored and sliced)
10	oz	pineapples (fresh or canned and drained)
12		strawberries (sliced)
1	cup	pecans (chopped)
1	cup	blueberries
1	cup	coconut (optional)

1. Fold whipped cream into yogurt and mix for about a minute or until fluffy.

2. Add all the fruits and pecans and mix well.

3. Refrigerate for at least 2 hours and it's ready to serve.

Fruit Salad Dressing

2		*egg yolks (beaten)*
1/2	*cup*	*sugar*
1/2	*tsp*	*salt*
1/4	*cup*	*lemon juice*
1	*tsp*	*lemon zest*
1	*tsp*	*vinegar*
1	*tsp*	*butter or virgin coconut oil*
1	*cup*	*heavy cream (whipped)*

1. Combine first 6 ingredients in a double boiler and cook until thick, stirring constantly.
2. Add butter and let cool.
3. Just before serving fold in whipped cream.
4. Serve on fruit.

French Dressing

1/4	*cup*	*tomato catsup*
3/4	*cup*	*olive oil or virgin coconut oil*
1	*tsp*	*salt*
1	*tsp*	*dry mustard*
1/4	*cup*	*vinegar*
1/4	*cup*	*sugar*
		paprika

1. Put catsup in a medium mixing bowl and add all dry ingredients.
2. Beat in oil gradually.
3. Add vinegar.

Variations: Add cheese, grated onion, garlic, etc.

Salad Dressing Made With Butter

4	*Tbsp*	*butter*
1	*Tbsp*	*flour*
1	*Tbsp*	*sugar*
1	*tsp*	*salt*
3		*eggs*
1	*tsp*	*mustard (heaping)*
1	*pinch*	*cayenne pepper*
1	*cup*	*milk*
1/2	*cup*	*vinegar*

1. Heat butter in a sauce pan. Add flour and stir until smooth.

2. Add milk and bring to a boil. Stir constantly.

3. Beat eggs, salt, pepper and mustard together in a bowl.

4. Beat vinegar slowly into dry ingredients.

5. Add to boiling mixture and stir until it thickens. Remove from heat and stir for 5 more minutes.

Spinach Salad With Figs & Bacon Dressing

3	cups	spinach leaves
12		figs (washed)
1/4	cup	red onions (thinly sliced)
4	Tbsp	blue cheese (crumbled)
2	Tbsp	pecans (halves or coarsely chopped)

Dressing

3	slices	bacon (cooked and crumbled)
1/3	cup	sugar
1/4	cup	cider vinegar
3	Tbsp	pomegranate juice
2	tsp	cornstarch
1	pinch	salt

1. Arrange the spinach leaves on four salad plates. Slice figs in half and arrange on the spinach. Sprinkle thinly sliced red onion over the spinach, then sprinkle with the cheese and pecans. Combine dressing ingredients in a saucepan and bring to a simmer. Remove from heat and let cool slightly.

2. Spoon some of the warm dressing over the salads, making sure each salad gets some of the bacon pieces.

Spicy Thai Minced Chicken Salad

		oil for deep-frying (not peanut or soy oils)
1	*lb*	*skinless, boneless chicken breasts or thighs*
1/2	*tsp*	*hot chili powder or cayenne pepper*
4	*tsp*	*granulated sugar*
1/2	*cup*	*lime juice (4 to 5 limes)*
2 1/2	*Tbsp*	*nam pla (fish sauce)*
1		*small, hot chile (seeded and minced)*
4	*tsp*	*fresh ginger (grated)*
1/2	*cup*	*roasted almonds (smashed)*
1/4	*cup*	*celery hearts (finely minced)*
1/2	*cup*	*celery leaves (firmly packed)*
1/4	*cup*	*cilantro leaves (firmly packed)*
1/4	*cup*	*mint leaves (firmly packed and shredded)*
4		*leaves green leaf lettuce*

1. Place several inches of oil in a wide pot on medium heat. Mince chicken coarsely. When oil has reached 300°F (148°C), lower the chicken, all at once, into the oil. Immediately stir with a spoon to break up clumps.

2. Cook until chicken just loses its pink. Pour chicken immediately into a colander. Let chicken drain for a moment. Place chicken in a mixing bowl. Add the chili powder and mix well to color chicken evenly. Add the sugar, lime juice, fish sauce, minced chile, ginger and almonds; toss vigorously to blend. Add celery heart, celery leaves, cilantro and mint, and toss gently (so as to keep the leaves fluffy).

3. Place the lettuce leaves on 4 serving plates and top each leaf with a quarter of the chicken mixture. Serve immediately.

Cole Slaw

3	*cups*	*cabbage (shredded)*
1		*carrots (shredded)*
1/2	*cup*	*raisins or other dried fruit (optional)*

Dressing:

1/2	*cup*	*homemade mayonnaise** *(see next page)*
1	*Tbsp*	*milk*
1	*Tbsp*	*cider vinegar*
1-2	*Tbsp*	*sugar or agave*
		salt and pepper to taste

1. Mix together the ingredients for the dressing in a small bowl.

2. Pour over cabbage and mix thoroughly.

3. Let stand in covered dish in refrigerator until ready to serve (not over 30 minutes).

* Most mayonnaise is made of soy oil, which is contraindicated.

Mayonnaise

2		*egg yolks*
1 1/2	*Tbsp*	*vinegar*
1	*tsp*	*mustard or 1/2 tsp dry mustard*
1/2	*tsp*	*salt*
1/2	*tsp*	*sugar*
2 1/2	*Tbsp*	*lemon juice*
1	*cup*	*olive oil or virgin coconut oil*

1. Use a hand blender to make this mayonnaise. It is the fastest, easiest way.

2. Place all ingredients in the order listed into a tall 2- or 3-cup container that the blender will just fit into.

3. Carefully insert blender into container, disturbing the ingredients as little as possible. Turn on the blender and keep it vertical for about 5 or 10 seconds. Gradually start tipping the blender so that more of the ingredients are being mixed. Continue to blend until mixed well, or about 1 minute.

4. Refrigerate and enjoy. Keeps up to 5 days.

Note: The quality of olive oil used affects flavor intensity in finished mayonnaise. Extra virgin olive oil gives a strong flavor; lighter-colored olive oil gives the great flavor with less intensity.

You can add other ingredients like spices, different kinds of vinegar, etc., to make your mayonnaise interesting.

Yogurt Salad Dressing

1/4	*cup*	*plain yogurt*
1	*Tbsp*	*fresh lemon juice*
1/2	*tsp*	*coarse salt*
1/4	*tsp*	*ground pepper*

1. In a medium bowl, whisk together yogurt and lemon juice; season with coarse salt and ground pepper.

2. Add vegetables and fruit to your liking.

Italian Salad Dressing

2		*garlic cloves*
3	*Tbsp*	*dried oregano*
6		*oil-packed anchovy fillets (rinsed and patted dry)*
1/3	*cup*	*red wine vinegar*
1	*cup*	*extra-virgin olive oil or virgin coconut oil*
1/2	*tsp*	*salt*
		coarsely ground black pepper

1. To prepare dressing, combine garlic, oregano and anchovy fillets in a food processor and pulse until pureed. Add vinegar; pulse a few more times.

2. With motor running, slowly add oils; process until dressing is emulsified. Alternatively, you can mix by hand with a whisk. The dressing will be thick. Add salt and pepper.

3. The dressing will keep refrigerated up to 2 weeks.

Fruit Salad With Lemon-Lime Dressing

1		*papaya (peeled, seeded, and cut into 1" chunks)*
2		*bananas (sliced 1/2" thick)*
1		*mango (peeled, stoned, and cut into 1" chunks)*
1	*cup*	*pineapple (1" chunked)*
1	*pint*	*strawberries (hulled and halved)*
2	*Tbsp*	*fresh lemon juice*
2	*Tbsp*	*fresh lime juice*
1	*Tbsp*	*dark rum (optional)*
2	*Tbsp*	*sugar (or to taste)*
1	*bunch*	*mint (leaves only, coarsely chopped)*
		tiny sprigs of mint for garnish

1. In a large glass serving bowl or picnic container, combine all the fruits and toss very gently to mix. Sprinkle the lemon and lime juices, rum (if using), sugar and mint over the top and again toss gently to mix.

2. Garnish with tiny mint sprigs before serving.

Basic Vinaigrette

1	*Tbsp*	*Dijon mustard*
1/4	*cup*	*balsamic vinegar*
		salt and pepper
3/4	*cup*	*extra virgin olive oil*

1. Whisk vinegar and mustard together in a medium bowl. Salt and pepper lightly.
2. Slowly add olive oil while whisking vigorously. Taste when about half the oil is incorporated and add additional salt and pepper to taste.

Helpful Tips:

You can substitute any acidic liquid for the balsamic vinegar, such as lemon or other citrus juice; many kinds of vinegar (white wine, red wine, sherry, cider); or even champagne. Avoid vinegars and other things with sulfites in them.

The mustard can be omitted, but it adds flavor and helps bind the oil and vinegar together for a short while. After an hour or so the mixture will separate. Just whisk it back together when you want to use it.

Chopped, pureed or roasted shallots blend in well, as does honey for a touch of sweetness. Fresh herbs, like basil, parsley, thyme and marjoram, are also good additions. Add some concentrated pomegranate juice for some color, taste and antioxidants. Other juices like raspberry, blackberry, etc., work well, too.

Although vinaigrettes are usually used as salad dressings, they can also be used as sauces for light foods such as fish, shellfish and chicken.

Pesto Salad Dressing

8		*cloves garlic*
1	*cup*	*extra virgin olive oil*
2	*cups*	*fresh basil (chopped)*
1	*cup*	*parsley*
2	*tsp*	*salt*
		pepper to taste

1. Place the garlic and 1/4 cup of the olive oil in a blender with some of the greens. Puree, adding oil a little at a time and then adding more greens.

2. Continue until all the greens have been processed to the consistency of mayonnaise.

3. Season with salt and pepper and put into a jar with a tight-fitting lid. It will keep in your refrigerator for several months.

Mustard Vinaigrette

1		*garlic clove (sliced in half)*
1	*tsp*	*Dijon mustard*
1	*Tbsp*	*balsamic vinegar*
		Salt and freshly ground black pepper
3	*Tbsp*	*olive oil or virgin coconut oil*
3	*cups*	*salad vegetables and fruits (no legumes)*

1. Rub the inside of a large wooden bowl with the garlic clove and then either discard the clove or save it for another use. Put the mustard in the bowl and whisk in the balsamic vinegar vigorously for about 10 seconds to get a creamy consistency. Season with salt and pepper, to taste.

2. Drizzle in the olive oil as slowly as possible with one hand while whisking as quickly as possible with the other hand to emulsify. Lay the salad vegetables on top of the dressing and toss just before serving.

Fruit Salad Dressing

2		*egg yolks (beaten)*
1/2	*cup*	*sugar*
1/2	*tsp*	*salt*
1/4	*cup*	*lemon juice*
1	*tsp*	*lemon rind (grated)*
1	*Tbsp*	*vinegar*
1	*tsp*	*butter or virgin coconut oil*
1	*cup*	*heavy cream (whipped)*

1. Combine all ingredients except butter and cream. Cook in a double boiler until thick, stirring constantly.

2. Add butter and cool.

3. Just before serving, fold in cream.

4. Serve on fruit.

Spinach, Mushroom, and Fennel Salad

3	qts	baby spinach (lightly packed)
3	large	eggs (hard-cooked and cut into wedges)
5	ozs	mushrooms (thinly sliced)
5	ozs	good-quality, thick-cut bacon
4	Tbsp	extra virgin olive oil
1	large	head fennel (trimmed and thinly sliced)
2 1/2	Tbsp	shallot (minced)
1 1/2	tsps	fresh thyme (roughly chopped)
2 1/2	Tbsp	sherry vinegar
2	tsps	Dijon mustard
		salt and pepper to taste

1. Combine spinach, eggs, and mushrooms in a large shallow serving bowl.

2. Cut bacon on the diagonal into strips about 1/4" thick and 1 1/2" long.

3. Cook bacon with 1/3 cup water in a large frying pan over medium heat, stirring occasionally, until water disappears, 8 to 12 minutes. Add oils and cook until bacon is light golden but still supple, 3 to 5 minutes more. Transfer bacon with a slotted spoon to paper towels to drain.

4. Add fennel to pan and cook, stirring occasionally, until slightly softened, about 2 minutes. Transfer with a slotted spoon to more paper towels.

5. Stir shallot and thyme into fat in pan and cook until softened, about 2 minutes.

6. Remove pan from heat and whisk in vinegar to de-glaze pan. Whisk in mustard, 1/2 teaspoon each salt and pepper, and 2 teaspoons water.

7. Add bacon and fennel to salad, pour dressing on top, and toss gently to coat. Season to taste with more salt and pepper.

Gouda Spinach Salad

4	*slices*	*bacon (cooked and drained)*
1	*cup*	*gouda cheese (grated)*
4	*cups*	*spinach (washed and torn)*
8		*mushrooms (thinly sliced)*
1	*cup*	*green onion (chopped)*
DRESSING		
1/4	*cup*	*olive oil or virgin coconut oil*
2	*Tbsp*	*lemon juice*
1	*clove*	*garlic (minced)*
1/2	*tsp*	*salt*
1/4	*tsp*	*dry mustard*
		pepper to taste

1. Cook the bacon and drain. Crumble and toss with the cheese in a small bowl.

2. Combine oil, lemon juice, garlic, salt, mustard and pepper in a small jar and shake to combine.

3. Place spinach in a large bowl and toss with mushrooms, green onion and bacon cheese mixture.

4. Toss with salad dressing.

Radicchio, Fennel and Arugula Salad

6	*cups*	*radicchio (shredded)*
2	*cups*	*fennel bulb (thinly sliced)*
1/2	*cup*	*walnuts (toasted and chopped)*
2/3	*cup*	*gorgonzola (crumbled)*
6	*cups*	*arugula (washed and well-spun dry)*

DRESSING

2	*Tbsp*	*balsamic vinegar*
1	*tsp*	*Dijon mustard*
1/3	*cup*	*extra virgin olive oil*
		salt and pepper

1. For dressing, whisk balsamic vinegar, mustard, salt, pepper in a small bowl. Add oil in stream, whisking until dressing is emulsified.

2. In a large bowl toss radicchio, fennel, walnuts, gorgonzola and dressing.

3. Arrange the arugula on serving plates then put the radicchio mixture on top.

Grilled Cheese Sandwich
(Monte Cristo Style)

1	*oz*	*cheddar cheese*
2	*slices*	*multigrain bread*
1 1/2	*tsp*	*butter*
1		*egg*
1	*Tbsp*	*milk*
1	*pinch*	*salt to taste*

1. In a small bowl, beat the egg until light with a fork or whisk. Add milk and beat to combine well.

2. Dip each slice of bread in the egg mixture on both sides.

3. Melt the butter in a skillet and cook bread for three minutes on one side, or until golden.

4. Turn one slice of bread over and place cheese on it. Place the other slice on the first cooked side down so that the cheese is between the cooked sides of the bread.

5. Cook until the bottom slice is golden on the bottom and then turn and cook the top slice until golden.

6. If making more than one, keep hot in a warm oven until all are ready.

Note: Add sliced ham, turkey or chicken for additional flavor. Also you can add some vanilla to the egg mixture. May serve with jelly.

Tuna Sandwich Spread

2	*cans*	*chunk tuna (drained, watch for soy in tuna!)*
1	*dollop*	*mayonnaise (homemade or non-soy based)*
2	*Tbsp*	*sour cream*
2	*Tbsp*	*Dijon mustard*
1	*Tbsp*	*lemon juice*
		onion powder to taste
1/2	*cup*	*Parmesan cheese*
		salt and pepper to taste
		veggies (finely chopped)
		(see instructions for suggestions)

1. Mix all ingredients together in a bowl.

2. Spread on good bread, like the new white whole wheat bread or, better yet some homemade multigrain bread. (Don't tell them it's healthy). Good bread makes a difference.

Veggie suggestions. Spinach, carrots, bell peppers, tomatoes, apples (I know, it's not a veggie), celery, zucchini, or any other veggie that isn't too strong or bitter.

Chicken, salmon, pork or turkey can also be substituted for the tuna.

CHAPTER 6

Soups & Stews

Soups are great for G6PD Deficient people, especially soups made with a good stock that includes the bones. Red blood cells are created in the bone marrow, so eating stocks made from bones helps keep people with G6PD Deficiency healthy.

Here's how to make a great stock:

Any meat, poultry or fish can be used for soup stock. Vegetables should be rough cut.

Add scraps of meat, poultry or fish, including some of the flesh and bones, to a large pot of boiling water.

Add onions and garlic to taste.

Add carrots, celery and any other vegetables you have in the refrigerator that you need to use.

Season with salt and pepper and perhaps a bay leaf or two.

Cover and simmer until the chicken falls off the bones (about 1 1/2 hours). Strain the stock and refrigerate. The fat can be removed easily after it cools because it will solidify on top of the stock. Freeze what you aren't going to use within a couple of days.

DO NOT SUBSTITUTE MARGARINE FOR BUTTER!

Old Fashioned Chicken and Dumplings

4		chicken breasts, or 1 whole chicken

DUMPLINGS

2	cups	all-purpose flour
2	tsp	baking powder
5	Tbsp	butter
1	tsp	salt
1	cup	milk or cream
2		eggs

1. In a large pot, add chicken, cover with water and cook until tender. Salt and pepper to taste.

2. When tender (about 1-1/2 hours), remove chicken and strain broth. Add more water and bring to a boil.

3. Remove chicken from bones, cut into small pieces and add back to broth.

4. Whisk together first four dumpling ingredients in a medium bowl and add milk and eggs, stirring to form a stiff dough.

5. Roll out on floured pastry board as thin as possible (so the dough is almost see through).

6. Cut into one inch strips; pinch off 1- to 2-inch pieces and drop one at a time into boiling broth.

7. Stir very lightly to keep from sticking. Cover and cook on low heat for 10 minutes, stirring gently about 3 times.

Alternatively you can form dumplings with a spoon and drop them into the hot stock.

Slow-Cooker Pork Stew

1	*lb*	*fingerling potatoes*
3	*ea*	*carrots (cut into 2-inch chunks)*
2	*stalk*	*celery (cut into 2-inch chunks)*
3	*cloves*	*garlic (minced)*
2	*inch*	*piece of ginger (peeled and grated)*
1/3	*cup*	*all-purpose flour*
		Kosher salt and freshly ground pepper to taste
3	*ea*	*bay leaves*
1	*ea*	*bone-in pork shoulder or pork sirloin roast (2 to 2 1/2 lbs.)*
1	*tsp*	*dried thyme*
1/2	*tsp*	*dried oregano*
1/2	*tsp*	*ground allspice*
1	*ea*	*14 oz can diced tomatoes*

1. Combine the potatoes, carrots, celery, garlic and ginger in a slow cooker. Toss in half of the flour and season with salt and pepper. Scatter the bay leaves over the vegetables.

2. Season the pork generously with salt and pepper, sprinkle with the thyme, oregano and allspice and toss with the remaining flour to coat. Place the pork over the vegetables in the slow cooker. Add 2 cups water and the tomatoes, cover and cook on low 8 hours.

3. Discard the bay leaves. Remove the pork roast and slice or pull the meat off the bone into large pieces. Serve in bowls with the vegetables and broth.

Serves 4.

Slow-Cooker Cioppino

2		large onions (chopped)
2		medium stalks celery, (finely chopped)
5		cloves garlic, (finely chopped)
28	oz	canned tomatoes (undrained)
8	oz	bottle clam juice
6	oz	can tomato paste
1/2	cup	water
1	Tbsp	red wine vinegar
1	Tbsp	olive oil
2 1/2	tsps	Italian seasoning
1/4	tsp	sugar
1/4	tsp	crushed red pepper flakes
1		bay leaf
1	lb	fish, white, firm (cut into 1-inch pieces)
3/4	lb	shrimp (uncooked peeled, de-veined)
1	can	chopped clams (with juice, undrained)
1	can	crab meat (drained)
1/4	cup	fresh parsley (chopped)

1. In 5- to 6-quart slow cooker, mix all ingredients except fish, shrimp, clams, crab meat and parsley.
2. Cover; cook on high heat setting 3 to 4 hours.
3. Stir in fish, shrimp, clams and crab meat. Reduce heat setting to low. Cover.
4. Cook 30 to 45 minutes longer or until fish flakes easily with fork. Remove bay leaf. Stir in parsley.

New England Clam Chowder

2	*cans*	*clams (6.5 oz cans)*
1/2	*lb*	*bacon (cooked and diced)*
2	*Tbsp*	*all purpose flour*
5		*medium potatoes (diced)*
2		*carrots (diced)*
1	*cup*	*leeks (diced)*
		salt and pepper to taste
1	*quart*	*half-and-half*

1. Cook bacon until crisp and browned in a large soup pot. Remove the bacon and leave the drippings in the pot.

2. Add the potatoes and carrots to the bacon fat, season with salt and pepper and cook for five minutes on medium heat.

3. Add the leeks and cook another minute, stirring constantly.

4. Pour the juice from the clams into the pot and add enough water to just cover the potatoes, cover and cook until the potatoes and carrots are tender, 10 to 15 minutes.

5. Add the flour to a cup of the half-and-half and stir until well mixed and no lumps remain. Add all remaining ingredients to the pot and the flour mixture last. Stir until the chowder returns to a simmer and thickens.

Caribbean Fish Chowder

1/4 lb small shrimp
1/2 lb fish fillets
1/4 lb clams
3 cups fish stock
1 cup clam juice
1/2 cup burgundy wine
1 Tbsp olive or virgin coconut oil
3 cloves garlic (crushed)
3 stalks celery (diced)
1 potato (peeled & diced)
1/3 cup tomatoes (stewed and chopped)
1 green bell pepper (diced)
1/2 tsp basil
1/2 tsp oregano
2 bay leaves
1 tsp paprika
1/2 tsp celery seed
1/2 tsp dry mustard
1/2 tsp cilantro (dried)
salt and pepper to taste

1. Heat the oil in a large soup pot.

2. Saute the onion and garlic until the onions are translucent. Add all of the other ingredients except the shrimp, clams and the fish.

3. Simmer for 1 hour or until the vegetables are tender. Add the seafood and cook for 7 to 10 minutes at a low boil.

Leek and Potato Soup

8		*leeks (white and green part only)*
1	*stick*	*butter or virgin coconut oil*
4		*medium potatoes (peeled and finely diced)*
1		*carrot (thinly sliced)*
4	*cups*	*chicken broth (heated)*
1	*cup*	*milk*
		salt and white pepper to taste
		chopped parsley (garnish)

1. Cut leeks in half lengthwise and then crosswise in 1-inch pieces. Simmer gently in butter for about 10 minutes.

2. Add potatoes, carrot, chicken broth and water. Season with salt and white pepper to taste.

3. Cook over just enough heat to keep soup at low boil for 40 minutes or until potatoes can be mashed easily against sides of pan.

4. Let cool slightly and put through blender.

5. Return to stove. Stir in scant cup of milk. Adjust seasonings.

6. Garnish each serving with chopped parsley.

West African Chicken Soup

1 1/2	lbs	*chicken (cut up)*
1		*onion (chopped)*
1	lb	*mushrooms (chopped)*
1		*bunch collard greens or spinach*
6	ozs	*tomato paste*
		West African red pepper
		salt

1. Put chicken, onion and mushrooms in soup pot. Add enough water to just barely cover ingredients. Turn on medium-high heat. Cover and cook while you're washing and chopping the greens, about 10 minutes.

2. Stem and chop greens.

3. Add salt, red pepper and tomato paste. Boil for about another 5 or 10 minutes.

4. Add greens and replace lid, steaming greens and stirring them in.

Serve by itself or over rice.

Cream of Mushroom Soup

1	*lb*	*fresh mushrooms*
1/4	*cup*	*butter or virgin coconut oil*
2		*whole shallots (minced)*
2	*cups*	*milk*
1	*cup*	*heavy cream*
4		*egg yolks*
1/2	*cup*	*sherry or chicken stock*
		salt
		black pepper

1. Clean mushrooms, separating caps and stems. Slice half of the caps crosswise into 1/8-inch slices. Chop stems and remaining caps.

2. Melt 2 tablespoons butter in an enameled or stainless steel skillet and saute the sliced caps until they just turn color, about 5 minutes. Remove from skillet. Add 2 tablespoons butter to skillet and saute chopped mushrooms and shallots until just tender, about 10 minutes.

3. Combine chopped mushrooms and shallots with milk in a medium saucepan. Season with salt and pepper to taste. Simmer 20 to 25 minutes.

4. Beat egg yolks until light and lemon colored. Whisk cream into eggs. Whisk 1/2 cup of hot soup mixture into egg-cream mixture, 2 tablespoons at a time. Then blend egg mixture into the rest of the soup, pouring in a slow, steady stream, and beating constantly. Add sherry and heat through, but do not allow to boil.

Cream of Chicken Soup

1/2	cup	butter or virgin coconut oil
1		medium onion (chopped)
2		stalks celery (with leaves, chopped)
3		carrots (chopped)
1/2	cup	plus 1 tablespoon flour
7	cups	chicken broth
3		sprigs parsley
3		sprigs thyme
1		bay leaf
2 3/4	cups	cooked (diced chicken)
1/2	cup	heavy cream
2 1/2	tsp	dry sherry (optional)
1	Tbsp	sea salt or to taste
		black pepper to taste
2	Tbsp	flat-leaf parsley (chopped)

1. Put butter, onion, celery, and carrots in a large soup pot and cook, covered, stirring occasionally, until soft. Add the flour and cook, stirring constantly for 2 minutes more.

2. Add the broth and bring to a boil while stirring constantly. Tie the parsley sprigs, thyme, and bay leaf together with a piece of kitchen twine and add to the soup. Lower the heat and simmer for 15 minutes.

3. Stir in the chicken and bring to a boil. Remove from the heat.

4. Add heavy cream, sherry, salt and pepper while continuing to stir. Remove and discard the herb bundle.

Spring Greens Soup

2	*Tbsp*	*olive oil or virgin coconut oil*
1		*large onion (chopped)*
1		*large fennel bulb (chopped)*
1/2		*pound dandelion greens*
1/2		*pound mustard greens*
1/2		*pound baby spinach leaves*
4		*garlic cloves*
6	*cups*	*chicken broth*
1/4	*tsp*	*freshly ground white pepper*
1/4	*tsp*	*salt*
1	*cup*	*half-and-half*

1. Saute the onions and fennel in a large soup pot until tender. Add the greens and continue to saute until the greens are wilted.

2. Add the rest of the ingredients and heat until hot. Do not boil.

Serve with a crusty bread.

CHAPTER 7

Breads

Multigrain breads are very good for you, and are a wonderful source of vitamins, protein and antioxidants.

As explained in *Chapter 4: Breakfast,* multigrain flour is highly recommended to boost nutritional value of your meals.

If your family has an aversion to 100% whole wheat bread, then breads made with a mixture of white flour and multigrain flour may be the perfect solution. Its lighter texture and its mild, nutty flavor is perfect for sandwiches, rolls, or your favorite quick bread recipes.

Helpful Tips:

If your dough rises too much after shaping into loaves, it will fall, become coarse and open grained, and your bread will be dry. If this should happen, it is better to remold.

If you are short on time, add extra yeast. It won't affect the flavor. Yeasty taste results only when bread is too warm during the rising period.

DO NOT SUBSTITUTE MARGARINE FOR BUTTER!

Orange Rolls

1	*cup*	*scalded milk*
1/2	*cup*	*butter*
1/3	*cup*	*sugar*
1	*tsp*	*salt*
1	*Tbsp*	*yeast*
1/4	*cup*	*water*
2		*eggs (well beaten)*
1/4	*cup*	*orange juice*
2	*Tbsp*	*orange peel (grated)*
5	*cups*	*flour*

1. Mix together milk, butter, sugar and salt in a large mixing bowl. Cool to lukewarm and add yeast and water. Add eggs, orange juice and orange peel. Beat well.

2. Add flour and mix to soft dough. Cover and let stand for 10 minutes.

3. Knead dough on lightly floured surface, place in greased bowl, cover and let rise in warm place about 2 hours.

4. Form into rolls and bake at 350°F (176°C) for 30 to 40 minutes or until firm.

Makes about 12 rolls.

Date Nut Bread

1	cup	chopped dates
1	tsp	baking soda
1	cup	boiling water
3	Tbsp	butter
1/2	cup	sugar
1		beaten egg
2	cups	flour (whole grain recommended)
1	tsp	baking powder
1/2	tsp	salt
1	cup	nuts (not peanuts)
1	tsp	vanilla

1. Sprinkle baking soda over dates. Add boiling water and butter and let cool.
2. Add sugar, beaten egg and stir.
3. Add flour, baking powder and salt and stir.
4. Add nuts and vanilla.
5. Bake in loaf pan at 350°F (176°C) for 50 to 60 minutes or until firm and shrinks away from sides of pan.
6. Makes one loaf.

Date Nut & Cheese Bread

3/4	*cup*	*boiling water*
1 3/4	*cup*	*flour (whole grain recommended)*
1	*tsp*	*baking soda*
1		*beaten egg*
3/4	*cup*	*chopped nuts (no peanuts)*
1/2	*lb*	*dates (cut fine)*
1/4	*tsp*	*salt*
1/2	*cup*	*sugar*
1	*cup*	*grated cheese*

1. Pour boiling water over dates and let stand 5 minutes.
2. Sift flour, salt, baking soda and sugar together.
3. Add egg, nuts, cheese and dates. Mix well.
4. Bake at 350°F (176°C) in a parchment paper lined 5" x 7" loaf pan for 50 to 60 minutes

French Bread

2 1/2	*cups*	*lukewarm water*
2	*Tbsp*	*soft butter*
1	*Tbsp*	*sugar*
2	*Tbsp*	*yeast*
7 1/2	*cups*	*flour*
1/2	*cup*	*cornmeal*
1	*Tbsp*	*salt*
		poppy seeds

1. Pour water into a mixer with a bread hook or large bowl. Add yeast and sugar and let stand for a few minutes.

2. Add half the flour and all the salt to the water and mix until well mixed. Add the butter and the rest of the flour, 1/2 cup at a time.

3. Turn out into a large bowl, cover and allow to rise until doubled in bulk.

4. Punch down and divide into 2 loaves. Form each loaf into an oblong shape and score top diagonally with a knife.

5. Pour cornmeal onto 2 cookie sheets and lay formed bread dough diagonally on them. Cover and allow to double in bulk.

6. Beat 1 egg and a little canned milk until well beaten. Brush on loaves and sprinkle with poppy seeds.

7. Bake for about 40 minutes or until golden brown at 350°F (176°C).

Corn Bread

2	*cups*	*cornmeal*
1/2	*cup*	*flour (whole grain recommended)*
1		*egg*
2	*tsp*	*salt*
2	*Tbsp*	*sugar*
2	*Tbsp*	*melted butter*
2 1/2	*tsp*	*baking powder*
1 2/3	*cup*	*milk (if buttermilk is used, add 1/2 tsp baking soda)*

1. Mix dry ingredients, add milk and stir well.
2. Add unbeaten egg, mix and add melted butter.
3. Pour into hot, well-greased pan and cook 20 minutes at 375°F (190°C) until a toothpick inserted into the middle comes out clean.

Bran Nut Bread

1		*egg*
1/2	*cup*	*sugar*
1	*cup*	*milk*
2	*Tbsp*	*melted butter*
1	*cup*	*oat bran*
2	*cup*	*flour (whole grain recommended)*
3	*tsp*	*baking powder*
1	*tsp*	*salt*
3/4	*cup*	*chopped nuts (no peanuts, optional)*

1. Beat egg and sugar until light.

2. Add milk, butter and bran. Sift flour with baking powder and salt.

3. Combine with nuts and add to first mixture.

4. Bake in loaf pan at 350°F (176°C) for 50 to 60 minutes or until golden brown.

Banana Nut Bread

1 3/4	*cup*	*flour (whole grain recommended)*
1 1/4	*tsp*	*baking powder*
1/2	*tsp*	*baking soda*
2/3	*cup*	*sugar*
3/4	*tsp*	*salt*
1/3	*cup*	*butter (room temperature)*
2		*eggs*
1/2	*cup*	*walnuts (no peanuts)*
3		*bananas*

1. Pre-heat oven to 350°F (176°C) and thoroughly grease a loaf pan. Sift flour and measure into bowl. Add baking powder, baking soda and salt. Sift twice.

2. With electric mixer on low speed, gradually add sugar to butter and beat until fluffy. Add 1 egg and mix on low speed and then increase speed to medium. Beat until smooth and light (about 30 seconds). Add second egg and again beat until smooth.

3. Add nuts and blend.

4. Peel fully ripe bananas and slice into a medium bowl and mash with blender or fork. Measure 1 cup.

5. Add the flour mixture alternately with banana pulp, about 1/2 of each at a time. Mix at low speed just to blend after each has been added.

6. Pour into pan, push batter up into corners. Bake for 55 minutes or until brown. Turn out onto rack and cool.

7. Note: For easier slicing, wrap in wax paper and keep overnight.

No Knead Rolls

3 1/2	*cups*	*flour (approximately)*
1	*cup*	*milk*
1	*Tbsp*	*yeast*
3	*Tbsp*	*sugar*
1/4	*cup*	*butter*
3/4	*tsp*	*salt*
2		*eggs*

1. Heat milk, sugar, salt and butter until well dissolved. Cool to lukewarm.

2. Combine beaten eggs and yeast to mixture, and add just enough flour to make a soft dough (no kneading, just stir). Cover and let rise about 1 hour, then punch down and let rise once more. Put into pans and let rise again doubled (about 1 to 1 1/2 hours).

3. Bake 20 minutes at 425°F (218°C).

Savory Dill Zucchini Bread

2 1/2	*cups*	*flour*
1	*Tbsp*	*sugar*
1/4	*tsp*	*salt*
2	*tsp*	*dill weed*
1	*Tbsp*	*yeast*
3/4	*cup*	*milk*
1/4	*cup*	*butter*
1/2	*cup*	*zucchini, grated and drained*
1/2	*cup*	*ricotta cheese*
1		*egg*

1. In a large bowl, combine 1 cup flour, sugar, salt, dill weed, and yeast; blend well.

2. In a small saucepan, heat milk and butter until warm and add zucchini, cheese and egg; add to flour mixture.

3. Blend on low speed until moistened, and then beat an additional 2 minutes on medium.

4. Stir in remaining flour by hand to form a stiff batter.

5. Spoon into greased 1 1/2 quart casserole dish and cover loosely with oiled plastic srap and cloth towel. Let rise in a warm place until light (about 30 minutes).

6. Bake 30 to 40 minutes at 350°F (176°C).

Prune Bread

1	*cup*	*prunes*	*4*	*cups*	*flour (whole grain recommended)*
2	*cups*	*sugar*			
1	*tsp*	*cinnamon*	*2*	*tsp*	*baking soda*
1	*tsp*	*allspice*	*2*		*eggs, beaten*
1/4	*tsp*	*nutmeg*	*1*	*tsp*	*pepper*
1	*tsp*	*salt*	*1/2*	*tsp*	*baking powder*
3/4	*cup*	*butter*	*1*	*pinch*	*salt*

1. Soak prunes over night in enough water so that 2 cups will be left for the bread.
2. Remove prunes from water, chop and pit them.
3. Combine water, prunes, butter and baking soda. Boil 5 minutes and cool.
4. Add beaten eggs.
5. Sift flour and salt, add to mixture and combine well.
6. Bake in 2 well greased bread pans about 1 hour at 350°F (176°C).

Substitution: To make apricot bread, cut dried apricots in their skins using scissors. DO NOT SOAK. Otherwise, make as the prune bread.

Bread can be kept for several weeks in the refrigerator if tightly wrapped in foil.

White Rolls

7	*cups*	*flour*
1	*pint*	*milk*
3	*Tbsp*	*butter*
3	*Tbsp*	*sugar*
1	*Tbsp*	*yeast*
3	*tsp*	*salt*

1. Heat milk and add butter, sugar, salt and stir until dissolved. Cool to lukewarm.

2. Add yeast and enough flour to make a medium stiff dough. Knead about two minutes or until smooth.

3. Place in greased bowl, moisten top with warm water and cover. Let stand in warm place for about 1 1/2 hours or until double in bulk.

4. Shape into rolls or two loaves. Cover and let stand until double in bulk.

5. Bake in 350°F (176°C) oven until browned.

6. Remove from oven and grease with butter.

Substitutions: Whole wheat or multigrain flour may be substituted for 1/3 of the flour.

Apple Cranberry Muffins

1 3/4	cups	flour (whole grain recommended)
1/4	cup	sugar
1 1/2	tsps	baking powder
1/2	tsp	baking soda
1/2	tsp	salt
1		egg
3/4	cup	milk
3/4	cup	applesauce
1/4	cup	butter (melted)
1	cup	fresh cranberries (coarsely chopped)
2	tsps	flour (for cranberries)

TOPPING:

1/4	cup	sugar
1/2	tsp	ground cinnamon

1. In medium bowl, combine 1 3/4 cups of flour, 1/4 cup sugar, the baking powder, baking soda and salt.

2. In small bowl, combine egg, milk, applesauce and butter. Mix well.

3. Add egg mixture to flour mixture, stirring just until moistened. Batter will be lumpy.

4. In small bowl, toss cranberries with 2 tablespoons flour. Fold into batter.

5. Spoon batter into 12 greased 2 1/2" muffin cups. (Do not use muffin cups, as the paper will stick to the muffin when you try to peel it off to eat.)

6. In another small bowl, combine 1/4 cup sugar and the cinnamon. Sprinkle over muffins.

7. Bake in preheated 400°F (204°C) oven 20-25 minutes or until wooden pick inserted in center comes out clean. Remove from pan. Cool on wire rack.

CHAPTER 8

Vegetables & Side Dishes

If you make your vegetables interesting, your family will eat more of them. Make your meals colorful and they will be more nutritious.

Personally, being a guy, eating my vegetables was never my strong point. I wish I had discovered them much earlier in life. Perhaps I would have been much healthier.

We have tried to find recipes that would give you some ideas about how to make veggies tasty for those of us who do not take to them naturally. For more ideas on creative ways to disguise veggies for your picky eaters, see *Chapter 3: Feeding Babies and Children.*

One thing I have started doing is adding veggies to dishes like potatoes. Most people like potatoes, so I add squash, sweet potatoes, spinach, etc to them and it makes the dish a lot healthier. Add veggies to other dishes in small amounts at first and slowly increase them.

The list of veggies below are all good for building red blood cells. Remember to make your dishes colorful so you get all the vitamins you need.

artichokes
asparagus
broccoli
cabbage
corn
mushrooms
okra
peppers, raw
potatoes
pumpkin
spinach
summer squash
sweet potatoes
winter squash

Spinach Souffle

1	*Tbsp*	*butter or virgin coconut oil*
1	*Tbsp*	*all-purpose flour*
1	*cup*	*milk*
		salt and pepper to taste
1/2	*cup*	*cheese (grated)*
1/2	*tsp*	*salt*
1	*cup*	*spinach (minced, cooked and drained)*
3		*eggs*

1. Make a white sauce by melting the butter in a sauce pan and adding the flour. Stir constantly for about a minute on medium low heat.

2. Add the milk, stir and continue to cook until sauce thickens.

3. Add the cheese and salt. When melted add the spinach and the well-beaten egg yolks. Cool.

4. Fold in the beaten whites of the eggs and bake in a casserole for 30 minutes at 350°F (176°C).

5. Serve immediately.

Quick Candied Yams

5		*medium yams (washed)*
3/4	*cup*	*orange*
4	*Tbsp*	*butter or virgin coconut oil*
3/4	*cup*	*brown sugar*

1. Microwave the potatoes until done but not too soft. Cool slightly and peel. Cut in half lengthwise and place in a baking pan large enough for them to lay flat and separate.

2. Boil together the remaining ingredients until it forms a thin syrup.

3. Pour 1/3 of the syrup over the yams and place in a 350°F (176°C) oven until lightly browned.

4. Baste occasionally with the remaining syrup.

Cabbage Rolls

1	*head*	*cabbage (separated)*
1	*lb*	*lean ground beef*
1		*small onion*
1/2	*cup*	*rice*
1		*green bell pepper (chopped fine)*
		salt and pepper to taste
1/2	*Tbsp*	*butter or virgin coconut oil*

1. Place cabbage into boiling salted water for 5 minutes. Remove and drain.

2. Mix beef, onion, rice, butter and bell pepper and season with salt and pepper.

3. Place 1 or 2 tablespoons of the mixture in a cabbage leaf, and roll and secure with a toothpick.

4. Steam on a rack in a covered pan with 2 cups of salted water for 1 hour.

Carrots Supreme

2	*cups*	*carrots (cooked and cubed)*
3/4	*cup*	*liquid from drained carrots*
1 1/2	*Tbsp*	*flour*
1 1/2	*Tbsp*	*butter or bacon drippings*
1		*bell pepper (chopped)*
1		*small onion (chopped)*
4	*Tbsp*	*cream*
4	*Tbsp*	*buttered bread crumbs*
		salt and pepper to taste

1. Cook onion and pepper in butter until soft. Add flour and juice from carrots. Stir until no lumps remain.

2. Add cream.

3. Add carrots to a baking dish and cover with cream mixture.

4. Sprinkle with bread crumbs and bake in 375°F (190°C) oven for 20 minutes, or until brown.

Baked Squash

4		*medium squash (yellow or green)*
1/2		*onion (chopped fine)*
1 1/2	*cups*	*milk*
2	*Tbsp*	*butter or virgin coconut oil*
1	*cup*	*cheese (grated)*
		salt and pepper to taste

1. Cut squash into small pieces and boil with onion in salted water. Drain.

2. Mash squash slightly with butter, milk, cheese, salt and pepper. Bake in a 350°F (176°C) oven for 30 minutes.

Twice-Baked Potatoes Supreme

6		*large baked potatoes*
1/2	*cup*	*butter or virgin coconut oil*
1	*cup*	*cheddar cheese (grated)*
1	*cup*	*sour cream or unflavored yogurt*
1/2	*cup*	*ricotta cheese*
1	*Tbsp*	*Parmesan cheese*
		salt and pepper to taste
2	*Tbsp*	*parsley flakes*
2	*Tbsp*	*green onions or chives*
1	*cup*	*mushrooms (sliced)*
1	*cup*	*spinach (chopped)*
		dash of Tabasco sauce

1. Bake potatoes until very tender. Remove from oven and set aside to cool enough to handle.

2. Cut in half lengthwise and carefully scoop potato out so not to tear skins.

3. Place skins in a large baking pan and set aside.

4. In a large bowl add butter, cheddar cheese, sour cream, ricotta cheese, Parmesan cheese, salt, pepper, Tabasco sauce.

Vegetable Cheese Skillet

2	Tbsp	butter or virgin coconut oil
1/4	cup	bell peppers (finely chopped)
1/2	cup	onions (finely chopped)
3/4	cup	celery (finely chopped)
1	cup	mushrooms (sliced)
		salt and pepper to taste
3	cups	egg noodles (cooked)
1 1/4	cup	buttermilk
3	tsp	parsley
2	cups	cheddar cheese (shredded)
	dash	garlic powder

1. Heat butter in a skillet over medium heat until bubbly and hot; add vegetables (except mushrooms) and garlic powder and saute until vegetables are tender, about 5 minutes.

2. Add mushrooms, salt and pepper and continue to saute. Stir occasionally and cook for about 2 minutes.

3. Add noodles, milk, and parsley. Stir to combine thoroughly.

4. Sprinkle with cheese and transfer to broiler. Broil until cheese is melted. Make 6 servings.

Carrots and Onions

2	*cups*	*carrots (diagonally sliced)*
1	*cup*	*pearl onions*
1 1/2	*cups*	*water*
2	*Tbsp*	*butter or virgin coconut oil*
2	*tsp*	*cornstarch*
1/4	*tsp*	*salt*
	dash	*pepper*
1/2	*cup*	*orange juice*
2	*Tbsp*	*honey*
1	*Tbsp*	*parsley (chopped)*

1. In a small saucepan with a little water, bring carrots and onions to a boil. Cover. Cook until carrots are tender.

2. Drain and place in a serving dish. Melt butter in saucepan.

3. Stir together cornstarch, salt, pepper, orange juice and honey; blend well. Add to butter.

4. Cook until mixture boils and thickens, stirring constantly. Pour over carrots and onions. Sprinkle with parsley.

Broiled Summer Squash with Cheese

summer squash (yellow or zucchini)

butter or virgin coconut oil

cheese (shredded)

mozzarella cheese (grated)

salt and pepper to taste

pizza seasoning

1. Slice squash about 3/8 inch thick, lengthwise and put on a cookie sheet in a single layer.

2. Brush with melted butter and sprinkle with cheeses.

3. Season with salt and pepper to taste. Sprinkle with pizza seasoning.

4. Turn oven to broil and place cookie sheet on top rack and cook until cheese just starts to brown.

5. Serve immediately.

Cabbage & Apple Casserole

1	*small*	*head green cabbage*
1	*small*	*head red cabbage*
1	*cup*	*green bell pepper (minced)*
3	*cups*	*diced apples*
1/2	*cup*	*brown sugar*
		juice of one lemon
1/2	*cup*	*butter or virgin coconut oil*
		salt, pepper and nutmeg

1. Grind red and green cabbage separately.

2. Season red cabbage with salt and pepper and place in greased casserole. Dot with butter.

3. Add sugar, lemon juice and nutmeg to apples and place on top of cabbage.

4. Mix green cabbage with green pepper, season, place over apples. Dot with butter.

5. Cover with buttered bead crumbs and bake in 375°F (191°C) oven for about 25 minutes.

Makes about 6 to 8 servings.

Sam's Mashed Potatoes

3		*medium potatoes*
1		*medium sweet potato or yam*
1/4	*cup*	*milk*
1/4	*cup*	*butter or virgin coconut oil*
		salt & pepper to taste
		chives (chopped)

1. Peel potatoes and cut into 1/2 inch cubes. Put into a saucepan, cover with water and boil until tender.

2. Drain potatoes and mash with a potato masher. Add milk, butter and season. Combine well. Garnish with chives and serve immediately.

Uses For Cold Boiled Potatoes

1. Serve diced in white sauce with bread crumbs and butter or cheese on top. Brown top.

2. Dice 6 large potatoes and add chopped green pepper, onion, and 1 cup thin white sauce to which add 3/4 cup grated cheese, bread crumbs and butter on top. Bake in 375°F (191°C) oven for about 15 minutes or until top is brown.

3. Dice 6 large potatoes and turn in a skillet in which 4 tablespoons. salt pork, bacon or other grease has been heated. Press potatoes flat with a knife. Cook until browned on the bottom and then loosen and turn onto a plate. Place potatoes back in the pan with the unbrowned side down and cook until brown. Serve.

4. Shape cold mashed potatoes into cakes. Roll in flour. Brown in melted butter or bacon grease. Chopped parsley or celery may be added to potatoes.

5. Cut up potatoes into chunks and add to stews or soups at the last minute.

Macaroni and Cheese

16	oz	whole grain macaroni
1	Tbsp	olive oil
2	Tbsp	butter
1/2	cup	chopped onion
1		red pepper (finely diced)
1		orange pepper (finely diced)
1		zucchini (finely diced)
3	Tbsp	white or whole grain flour
12 oz	can	nonfat evaporated milk
1	cup	low sodium vegetable broth
1	cup	low fat cheddar cheese (shredded)
1	cup	Monterey jack cheese (shredded)
1/2	cup	almonds, dry roasted (chopped)
2	cups	seasoned croutons
		salt & pepper to taste

1. Cook macaroni according to package directions. Drain. Transfer to a large bowl and set aside.

2. Heat olive oil and butter in a large skillet over medium high heat. Add onion, peppers and zucchini. Cook until vegetables are soft, about 8 to 10 minutes. Season with salt and pepper.

3. Sprinkle flour over vegetables and stir until well combined. Add evaporated milk and vegetable broth. Bring to a boil, then turn down heat and let the mixture simmer until thickened, about 5 minutes.

4. Stir in cheeses until melted.

5. Pour vegetable cheese sauce over macaroni. Fold in until well combined. Transfer to greased 13” x 9” pan.

6. Put almonds and croutons in a food processor fitted with metal blade. Process until mixture is fine crumbs. Sprinkle on top of macaroni and cheese. Bake at 350°F (176°C) for 10 to 15 minutes until heated through.

Glazed Fall Vegetables

2		*large sweet potatoes*
1		*large russet potato*
1/2	*lb*	*baby carrots*
1		*acorn squash (peeled and cut into cubes)*
1/2	*cup*	*firmly packed brown sugar*
1/4	*cup*	*butter or virgin coconut oil (melted)*
1/4	*cup*	*sorghum*
1/4	*cup*	*water*
1/2	*tsp*	*salt*
1	*tsp*	*ground cinnamon*
1	*tsp*	*vanilla extract*

1. Cut potatoes in half lengthwise; cut into 1/2-inch thick slices.

2. Place potato slices, carrots, and squash in a lightly greased 13" x 9" baking dish.

3. Stir together sugar and remaining ingredients. Drizzle over potato mixture, tossing to coat.

4. Bake, covered, at 425°F (220°C) for 30 minutes. Uncover and gently stir vegetables. Bake 15 or 20 more minutes or until vegetables are tender.

Makes about 6 to 8 servings.

CHAPTER 9

Main Dishes

Because most people with G6PDD cannot eat legumes, they must get their protein from meats, poultry and sea food.

Poultry, meat and seafood provide nutrients necessary for the development of red blood cells, especially the bone marrow and liver. Liver should be on the menu on a regular basis, as should soup and other dishes made with bone stock.

When I was a young lad, I got sick with hepatitis, as did just about every other child in my school. I was fed only liver and grape juice and was back in school in a week, while other children were home sick for 6 weeks or more. I'm a believer in the benefits of liver. Once a week or so is just fine, unless you are experiencing hemolysis.

DO NOT SUBSTITUTE MARGARINE FOR BUTTER!

Beef Stroganoff

1 1/2	lbs	beef stew meat
1	Tbsp	olive oil or virgin coconut oil
2	cups	mushrooms (sliced)
1/2	cup	green onions (sliced)
2	cloves	garlic (minced)
1/2	tsp	dried oregano (crushed)
1/4	tsp	salt
1/4	tsp	dried thyme (crushed)
1/4	tsp	pepper
1	ea	bay leaf
2	cups	beef broth
1	cup	sour cream
1/3	cup	flour
1/4	cup	water

1. Cut up any large pieces of stew meat. In a large skillet, brown meat, half at a time, in hot oil.

2. In a 3 1/2- or 4-quart slow cooker place mushrooms, onions, garlic, oregano, salt, thyme, pepper, and bay leaf. Add stew meat. Pour beef broth over all.

3. Cover and cook on low-heat setting for 8 to10 hours or on high-heat setting for 4 to 5 hours. Discard bay leaf.

4. If using low-heat setting, turn to high-heat setting. In a bowl, whisk together sour cream, flour, and water until smooth. Stir about 1 cup of the hot liquid into sour cream mixture. Return all to cooker; stir to combine. Cover and cook about 30 minutes more or until thickened and bubbly.

5. If desired, serve over hot cooked pasta; sprinkle with parsley.

6. Serves 6.

Meat Loaf

1	lb	lean ground beef
1/2	lb	ground pork
1	tsp	salt
1/2	tsp	pepper
1/2	tsp	sage
1	Tbsp	vinegar
1		egg
1	small	onion (chopped)
1	small	carrot (grated)
1		bell pepper (chopped fine)
1 1/2	cups	bread crumbs
1	can	tomato sauce or salsa

1. Combine all ingredients, except tomato sauce, and put in a loaf pan. Cover with tomato sauce and bake in 300°F (148°C) oven for 1 1/2 hours.

Note: Add some ground liver and spinach to this dish for extra nutrition. (If you don't tell them, no one will know.)

Baker Tacos

This dish is prepared by putting seasoned raw ground beef inside the tortillas before frying them. They are then eaten with a fork full of fresh salad, cheese and homemade pico de gallo with every bite. These delicious (and very healthy) tacos will easily become a favorite meal for your family.

12		*fresh corn tortillas*
2	*lbs*	*lean ground beef*
		garlic salt
		pepper
		lard (enough for 3/8-inch grease in frying pan)
		pico de gallo (on the following page)

1. Prepare pico de gallo using recipe on following page. Can be prepared the previous day and kept covered in the refrigerator.

2. Prepare a salad of greens (use a variety), olives, diced tomatoes, onions, grated cheese (four cheese Mexican blend works well), peppers (hot, sweet or both). Add any other vegetables you like. Put the ingredients in separate bowls for serving.

3. Put lard into a large frying pan about 3/8-inch deep and heat on medium high until hot.

4. If tortillas are refrigerated, let stand at room temperature for an hour. Spread raw ground beef on 1/2 of the taco about 1/4-inch thick. Season with garlic salt and pepper. Cook in hot grease for about 5 seconds and then fold meat side over the side without meat. Fry until golden brown, turn over, and fry other side. Remove to a bowl lined with paper towels to drain. Continue until all tacos are fried.

Serving suggestions: Place tacos, salad ingredients and pico di gallo on table. Make a salad from the assortnment of veggies on one half of your plate, and top it off with cheese and pico de gallo. Eat the salad with the tacos.

Pico de Gallo

2		*medium tomatoes (diced)*
1/3	*cup*	*cilantro (chopped)*
3		*green onions (chopped)*
1		*clove garlic (minced)*
1		*small jalapeño (minced)*
1		*avocado (peeled, pitted and diced)*
1	*can*	*hearts of palm (15 oz drained and thinly sliced)*
1/4	*cup*	*orange juice*
2	*Tbsp*	*grated orange peel*
5	*cups*	*flour*
2	*Tbsp*	*fresh lime juice*
1/4	*tsp*	*sea salt*

1. Combine tomatoes, chopped cilantro, green onions, garlic and jalapeño in medium bowl.

2. Add remaining ingredients; gently toss to mix.

Pork Chops & Rice

6		*pork chops*
21/2	*cups*	*water*
12	*Tbsp*	*rice (uncooked)*
1		*onion*
3		*tomatoes*
		salt and pepper

1. Fry pork chops in virgin coconut oil until brown; place in a covered casserole.

2. Pour fat out of frying pan. Put water into frying pan and let simmer until cracklins are loose. Pour water and cracklins over pork chops.

3. Put 2 tablespoons of rice on each pork chop, then 1 onion slice, and a few tomato slices, salt and pepper.

4. Cook in 350°F (176°C) oven for 1 hour or until rice is done.

Pork Chops Delight

4		*pork chops*
1		*onion (sliced)*
1	*pkg*	*mixed vegetables (no legumes)*
1	*can*	*tomatoes (15 oz)*
1	*can*	*tomato sauce (small can)*

1. Brown pork chops in a little virgin coconut oil and place in a shallow pan. Put onions on top followed by vegetables. Pour tomatoes and tomato sauce over all. Salt and pepper to taste.

2. Bake uncovered for 1 hour in 350°F (176°C) oven.

3. Serve with baked potatoes.

Butterflied Chops with Sun Dried Tomato

4		*butterflied pork chops*
1	*tsp*	*olive or virgin coconut oil*
1		*clove garlic (finely chopped)*
3/4	*cup*	*chicken broth*
2	*Tbsp*	*white wine*
1 1/4	*cups*	*water*
1/4	*cup*	*evaporated milk*
3	*Tbsp*	*tomato paste*
2	*Tbsp*	*sun-dried tomato bits*
1 1/2	*tsps*	*dried basil leaves*
1	*tsp*	*sugar*
1/8	*tsp*	*pepper*
2	*Tbsp*	*cornstarch*
4	*cups*	*hot cooked pasta*

1. Prepare grill for medium direct heat. Brush grill with cooking oil. Place chops on cooking grill. Grill, covered, 12 to 15 minutes or until pork reaches an internal temperature of 160°F (71°C). Turn pork once during grilling.

2. In 10-inch nonstick skillet, heat oil over medium-high heat; sauté garlic. Add broth and wine to de-glaze pan. Add 1 cup water, milk, tomato paste, tomato bits, basil, sugar and pepper. Cook over medium heat, until sauce comes to a boil, stirring constantly.

3. Combine remaining 1/4 cup water and cornstarch; add to sauce. Cook over medium heat until sauce is thickened, stirring constantly.

4. Serve butterflied chops on bed of pasta topped with sauce.

Slow-Cooker Osso Buco

1/2	cup	all-purpose flour
4		veal shank (about 2" thick)
		salt and pepper
2	Tbsp	unsalted butter or virgin coconut oil
1	cup	dry white wine
1	can	diced tomatoes (14 1/2 oz)
3/4	cup	chicken broth
1	small	red onion (chopped)
1		carrot (peeled and sliced)
1	stalk	celery (chopped)
5	sprigs	fresh thyme
3	Tbsp	fresh parsley (finely chopped)
1	Tbsp	lemon zest (finely grated)
1	clove	garlic (minced)

1. Put the flour in a wide, shallow dish. Season the veal shanks all over with salt and pepper and dredge in the flour; shake off the excess flour.

2. Heat a 12-inch skillet over medium heat. Add the butter, and when it foams, add the shanks to the skillet. Cook until golden, turning once, about 10 minutes. Transfer the shanks to a slow cooker.

3. Add the wine to the skillet. Scrape up any browned bits from the bottom of the skillet and pour the contents of the skillet into the slow cooker. Add the tomatoes and their juices, chicken broth, onion, carrot, celery, and thyme. Cover and cook on low heat for 6 to 8 hours; the meat will be very tender and almost falling off the bone.

4. Transfer the shanks to a platter and cover with foil to keep warm. Pour the sauce from the slow cooker into a large skillet. Simmer over medium heat until reduced to about 2 cups, 10 to 15 minutes. Season to taste with salt and pepper.

5. Meanwhile, in a small bowl, combine the parsley, lemon zest, and garlic to make a gremolata. Serve the veal shanks topped with the sauce and the gremolata.

Fluffy Salmon Loaf

1	*can*	*pink salmon (wild caught is best)*
1/2	*tsp*	*salt*
1/4	*tsp*	*paprika*
1/4	*tsp*	*pepper*
2	*Tbsp*	*lemon juice (fresh squeezed)*
3		*eggs (separated)*
1/2	*cup*	*bread crumbs*
1/2	*cup*	*milk (hot)*

1. Remove skin and bones from salmon.

2. Mix together salmon, salt, paprika, pepper, lemon juice, beaten egg yolks, bread crumbs and hot milk.

3. Beat egg whites until stiff and fold into salmon mixture.

4. Pour into greased loaf pan and bake for 1 hour at 350°F (176°C).

Baked Salmon Roll

2	*cup*	*all purpose flour*
4	*tsp*	*baking powder*
3/4	*tsp*	*salt*
1/3	*cup*	*butter or virgin coconut oil*
3/4	*cup*	*liquid (half water half milk)*
1	*cup*	*salmon (flaked)*
1		*green pepper (chopped)*
2	*Tbsp*	*onion (chopped)*
1/2	*tsp*	*salt*
1/4	*tsp*	*pepper*

1. In a large bowl, mix together first 3 ingredients. Cut in butter with a pastry cutter.

2. Add liquid and stir until soft dough forms and follows the spoon around the bowl.

3. Place dough on a lightly floured board and knead lightly for 30 seconds. Roll into a 12" by 6" rectangle, 1/2" thick. Brush with melted butter.

4. Combine remaining ingredients and spread on dough.

5. Roll like cinnamon rolls and slice into 1 1/2-inch rolls using dental floss or a floured knife.

6. Place 1/2 inch apart in a pan and bake at 425°F (218°C) for 25 minutes or until lightly brown.

7. Serve hot plain or with egg or cheese sauce.

Poached Salmon

1	*lb*	*salmon fillets*
1/2	*cup*	*dry white wine*
1/2	*cup*	*water*
1		*small onion or shallot (sliced thin)*
		fresh or dried dill
		parsley
		pepper

1. Put wine, water, dill, parsley and onions in a saute pan, and bring to a simmer on medium heat.

2. Place salmon fillets, skin-side down on the pan. Cover. Cook 5 minutes or to desired doneness. Do not overcook.

3. Serve sprinkled with freshly ground black pepper.

Sesame Orange Shrimp

3	*Tbsp*	*sesame seeds (white or black or a mix)*
2		*large egg whites*
1/4	*cup*	*cornstarch*
1/4	*tsp*	*salt*
1/4	*tsp*	*freshly ground pepper*
1	*lb*	*peeled and de-veined raw shrimp (21-25 per pound)*
2	*Tbsp*	*olive oil or virgin coconut oil (divided)*
3/4	*cup*	*orange juice*
1/4	*cup*	*vermouth*
1	*tsp*	*sugar*
1		*scallion (thinly sliced)*

1. Whisk sesame seeds, egg whites, cornstarch, salt and pepper in a large bowl. Add shrimp and toss to coat.

2. Heat 1 tablespoon oil in a large nonstick skillet over medium heat. Add half the shrimp and cook until golden, 1 to 2 minutes per side. Transfer to a paper towel lined plate to drain. Repeat with the remaining 1 tablespoon oil and the rest of the shrimp.

3. Add orange juice, vermouth and sugar to the pan. Bring to a boil and cook, stirring occasionally, until slightly thickened and reduced by half, 4 to 6 minutes.

4. Return the shrimp to the pan and stir to coat with the sauce. Serve immediately, with scallion sprinkled on top.

Liver Casserole

1	*lb*	*calf's liver (cut into 1 inch squares)*
1	*cup*	*onions (chopped)*
1	*cup*	*celery (chopped)*
1	*cup*	*carrots (cooked)*
1	*can*	*tomato sauce*
1/2	*tsp*	*salt*
		pepper to taste
3	*Tbsp*	*flour*
1	*cup*	*cheddar cheese (grated)*

1. Season liver with salt and roll in flour. Brown slowly in a frying pan with a little butter or virgin coconut oil.

2. In another pan, brown onions, celery and then add the carrots, tomato sauce and salt (less salt if sauce is salted).

3. Put liver into a baking dish and add liquid mixture. Bake for 40 minutes in 350°F (176°C) oven.

4. Add grated cheese and bake 15 minutes longer.

Cassoulet

4		*bone-in chicken thighs*	*1/2*	*cup*	*white wine*
		salt and pepper	*2*	*cups*	*cooked brown rice*
1/2	*lb*	*slab bacon*	*1*		*bay leaf*
1	*large*	*onion*	*2*	*tsp*	*dried thyme*
3		*celery stalks*	*1/2*	*cup*	*chicken stock*
2		*carrots*	*1*		*tomato*
4		*garlic cloves*	*1*	*cup*	*bread crumbs*

1. Preheat the oven to 350°F (176°C). Rinse and dry the chicken well and season with salt and pepper. Let sit at room temperature 15 minutes.

2. In a large Dutch oven, over medium low heat, add the bacon and slowly render the fat. Remove the bacon to a plate when crispy, leaving the fat in the pan.

3. Raise the heat to medium-high and add the chicken, skin side down. Brown the chicken on both sides and then remove to a plate.

4. Add the onion, celery and carrots and saute until soft, about 5 minutes. Add the garlic and cook until fragrant, another minute.

5. De-glaze the pan with white wine and reduce by half. Stir in rice, bay leaf and thyme.

6. Nestle chicken thighs and bacon back into pot. Add the chicken stock, cover and bake in the oven for 35 minutes. During the last 15 minutes of cook time, remove the lid and cover the top with sliced tomatoes and the garlic bread crumbs.

Serve cassoulet with baguette.

Note: This is great with a few duck parts added to the chicken.

Baked Ziti

1	*can*	*whole tomatoes, (28 ounce peeled*
1	*Tbsp*	*olive oil or virgin coconut oil*
6		*garlic cloves (minced)*
1/4	*tsp*	*red pepper flakes*
		salt and pepper
3	*cups*	*water*
12	*ozs*	*ziti pasta*
1/2	*cup*	*heavy cream*
1	*oz*	*Parmesan cheese*
1/4	*cup*	*chopped fresh basil*
4	*ozs*	*mozzarella cheese (shredded)*

1. Preheat the oven to 475°F (246°C). Meanwhile, pour the whole can of tomatoes into a blender or food processor. Process until the tomatoes are roughly chopped, not pureed.

2. Pour the oil into a large oven-safe skillet set over medium-high heat. Add the garlic and red pepper flakes and cook for about 1 minute, or until fragrant.

3. Pour in the chopped tomatoes and 1/2 teaspoon of salt. Bring to a boil, then reduce the heat to medium-low and simmer for 10 minutes, stirring occasionally.

4. Pour in the water, stir, and then add the pasta. Turn the heat back up to medium-high. Cook until the pasta is tender, about 15 minutes.

5. Add the cream, Parmesan, and basil. Stir well. Season with salt and pepper to taste. Then sprinkle the mozzarella on top.

6. Place skillet in the oven and cook for 10 to 15 minutes, or until the cheese has melted and slightly browned.

Lamb Pot Pie

3	*Tbsp*	*all-purpose flour*
1	*tsp*	*salt*
1	*tsp*	*pepper*
2	*Tbsp*	*olive or virgin coconut oil*
2	*lbs*	*lamb (boneless leg or shoulder, cut into 1/2 inch cubes)*
1 1/2	*cup*	*chicken broth*
3		*cloves garlic (finely chopped)*
3/4	*tsp*	*dried dill*
3/4	*tsp*	*ground ginger*
3/4	*tsp*	*paprika*
1 1/4	*cups*	*vegetables (mixed, unfrozen)*
1/4	*cup*	*parsley (chopped)*
1		*double pie crust (see pie crust recipe in dessert chapter)*
1		*egg*
1	*Tbsp*	*water*

1. In plastic or paper bag, combine flour, salt and pepper. Add meat; shake to coat with flour; set aside.

2. In large skillet, heat oil and brown meat. Add broth, garlic, dill weed, ginger and paprika. Simmer for 10 minutes, stirring occasionally.

3. Mix in vegetables and parsley. Pour into 11” x 7” baking dish. Cool slightly.

4. Unfold pastry and fit over top of lamb mixture. Crimp edges and decorate as desired. Make several slits in pastry. Beat egg with 1 tablespoon water. Brush on pastry.

5. Bake at 400°F (204°C) for 25 to 30 minutes or until pastry is golden brown.

Lasagna

2	lbs	lean ground beef
2	Tbsp	olive oil
1		yellow onion (chopped)
3		cloves garlic (minced)
2	tsp	Italian seasoning to taste
		salt and pepper to taste
2	cans	tomato sauce (8 ounces)
2	cans	tomato paste (6 ounces)
2	cups	tomato juice
1	cup	water
2	lbs	fresh mushrooms, sliced
2		mozzarella cheese
1		Parmesan cheese
16	oz	ricotta cheese
3		eggs
1		package lasagna noodles

1. In a medium size bowl, mix ricotta cheese and egg together until creamy and set aside in refrigerator.

2. In a large skillet, saute onions and garlic in oil until onions are translucent. Add ground beef to skillet and brown. Add salt, pepper and Italian seasoning and mix well.

3. Stir in tomato sauce, tomato paste, tomato juice, water and mushrooms. Simmer for at least 1 hour. The longer the sauce simmers, the better the flavors blend.

4. While sauce simmers, prepare noodles according to package directions. Drain, cover with cold water and allow to cool. Do not drain cold water off noodles.

5. In a large baking pan, spread a thin layer of sauce in the bottom of pan. Arrange a layer of noodles, sauce, cheese mixture, mozzarella cheese, sprinkle with Parmesan cheese, noodles, sauce, cheese mixture, cheeses, etc. Continue layering, ending with thin layer of sauce and sprinkle with Parmesan cheese.

6. Bake at 350°F (176°C) for 45 minutes to 1 hour.

Options: Cooked and sliced Italian sausages may be added to sauce at the time you add mushrooms.

Serve with salad and garlic bread.

Serves 10 to 12.

Chicken Enchiladas

6		boneless skinless chicken breasts
1	tsp	garlic powder
1		yellow onion (finely chopped)
1	tsp	cumin
1	Tbsp	chili powder
1	cup	sour cream or plain yogurt
1	can	green chilies (chopped)
1		small can black olives (chopped)
		salt and pepper to taste
1	cup	red salsa
2	cups	cheddar cheese (grated)
2	cups	Monterey jack cheese (grated)
1		lemon
2	doz	corn tortillas

1. Combine chicken, garlic powder, onion, cumin, chili powder, salt, and pepper in large sauce pot cover with water and bring to boil.

2. Reduce heat and simmer until chicken is tender. Cool and drain water with colander or strainer so not to loose onion and spices.

3. Add remaining ingredients, except for cheeses and lemon, and mix well.

4. Spray a 13" x 9" baking pan with non-stick spray and set aside.

5. Heat tortillas on griddle or in microwave until soft and pliable.

6. Place 1 to 2 heaping tablespoons of filling and a little of the cheese (just a sprinkle of each) on tortilla and roll up. Place in baking pan. Continue procedure until all tortillas have been used.

7. Reserve a little of the filling to spread over the top of enchiladas. Sprinkle with remaining cheese. Squeeze the juice of 1 lemon over top of cheese.

8. Bake at 350°F (176°C) for 20 to 25 minutes or until cheese is melted.

Spaghetti

1	*lb*	*ground beef*
8	*oz*	*tomato sauce (organic if possible)*
1/2	*small*	*onion (mild)*
1/2		*bell pepper (finely chopped)*
1	*small*	*carrot (finely chopped or pureed)*
1/4	*cup*	*spinach (finely chopped or pureed)*
		salt and pepper to taste
		powdered garlic to taste
		Parmesan cheese (optional)
		parsley to taste
8	*oz*	*spaghetti*

1. Cook carrots in a pot with a little water until tender.

2. Brown ground beef in a skillet. Add onions and cook for 1 or 2 minutes more. Drain most of the fat from the skillet.

3. Add peppers, carrots, spinach and powdered garlic and reduce heat. Cook for a minute or two.

4. Add tomato sauce. Reduce heat to a simmer. Cover and cook until vegetables are tender.

5. Add spaghetti to a pot of salted boiling water and cook about 20 minutes until tender.

6. Serve meat sauce and spaghett separetly, or mix together. Serve with Parmesan cheese.

Note: Be creative with this. The spaghetti sauce will mask many flavors. A small amount of finely chopped liver or lamb can be substituted for the ground beef. Try a variety of veggies like squash, greens, etc. Other spices can be added, depending on your child's tastes.

Calf's Liver with Grapes

1	*lb*	*calf's liver (cut 1/4-inch thick slices)*
1/2	*tsp*	*salt*
1/4	*tsp*	*pepper*
1/4	*cup*	*flour*
1/4	*cup*	*butter or virgin coconut oil*
1/3	*cup*	*chicken broth*
2	*lbs*	*seedless green grapes*

1. Salt and pepper liver. Dredge with flour. In large, heavy skillet, heat 2 tablespoons butter. Add liver, and cook for 2 minutes each side. Remove liver to heated dish and keep warm. Pour fat off skillet.

2. Add chicken broth to skillet and cook over brisk flame, scraping the bottom of the skillet until the brown crust is dissolved. Bring to boil. Return liver to skillet. Cover. Simmer gently for 5 minutes.

3. Meanwhile, stem and wash grapes. In small skillet, heat remaining butter. Add grapes to skillet and cook for 5 minutes, or until grapes are golden brown.

4. Remove grapes and arrange in center of heated serving dish. Surround grapes with slices of liver. Pour sauce from liver skillet over slices.

Healthier Hamburger

1	lb	lean hamburger
4	ozs	liver (finely chopped, lamb may be substituted)
1		egg
1/2	cup	multigrain bread crumbs
1/2	cup	spinach (pureed or very finely chopped carrots, cauliflower, squash or other veggie can be substituted or added)
1/4	cup	mild onion (finely chopped)
2	Tbsp	catsup
		salt and pepper to taste

1. Mix all ingredients together in a bowl. Let sit in the refrigerator for 15 minutes.

2. Form into patties and grill or saute.

3. Serve on multigrain hamburger buns and top with cheese and your favorite condiments.

Note: You can be very creative with this. (If McDonald's can add soy to their hamburgers and the kids love them, then they will like these just as well.) Start out with smaller amounts of veggies, and gradually add more.

You can use this mixture to make meat loaf, or used in place of plain hamburger in many recipes.

Khoresht Anar-Aveej

1-1.5	*kgs*	*chicken pieces*
500	*grams*	*ground walnuts*
2	*Tbsp*	*rice flour*
500	*grams*	*parsley, mint, coriander, spring onion ends*
3-4		*onions*
2-3	*cloves*	*garlic*
3-4	*cups*	*pomegranate juice*
2-3	*Tbsp*	*sugar*
1/2	*cup*	*virgin coconut oil*
		salt to taste

1. Peel onions and slice thinly. Fry in oil until slightly golden. Wash chicken pieces and fry in onions until color changes. Add 3 glasses of hot water and bring to boil. Turn heat down and let boil slowly for about 30 minutes adding more hot water if needed.

2. Wash and rinse the herbs, then finely chop them. Peel garlic cloves and thinly slice them. Fry herbs and garlic in oil for a few minutes.

3. Add herbs, salt, ground walnuts and pomegranate juice or paste (if using pomegranate paste, add 2 more glasses of hot water and bring to slow boil). If pomegranate juice or paste is sour, add some sugar to the khoresht. Dissolve rice-flour in a cup of cold water and add to khoresht near the end of cooking.

Notes: Care should be taken to cook the khoresht long enough so that the oil in walnuts comes out and the mix becomes quite thick. Khoresht anaar-aveej should be served with white rice.

Pork or Chicken Adobo
(Philippines)

1/2 kilo pork cut in cubes + 1/2 kilo chicken, cut into pieces, or choice of either 1 kilo pork or 1 kilo chicken

1	*head*	*garlic (minced)*
1/2		*yellow onion (diced)*
		ginger to taste (optional)
1/4	*cup*	*fish sauce**
1	*cup*	*vinegar*
2	*cups*	*water*
1	*tsp*	*paprika*
5		*laurel leaves (bay leaves)*
4	*Tbsp*	*virgin coconut oil*
2	*Tbsp*	*cornstarch*
		salt and pepper (to taste)
3	*Tbsp*	*water*

* The traditional soy sauce is replaced with fish sauce in this recipe.

1. In a big sauce pan or wok, heat 2 tablespoons of oil, then sauté the minced garlic and onions.

2. Add the pork and chicken to the pan. Add 2 cups of water, 1/8 cup of fish sauce, vinegar, paprika and the bay leaves. Bring to a boil. Cover and simmer for 30 minutes or until meat is tender.

3. Remove the pork and chicken from the saucepan and in another pan, heat cooking oil and brown the pork and chicken for a few minutes.

4. Mix the browned pork and chicken back into the sauce and add cornstarch dissolved in water to thicken. Add salt and/or pepper if desired.

5. Bring to a boil then simmer for an additional 5 minutes. Serve hot with the adobo gravy and rice.

Arroz Caldo
(Philippines)

1	*kilo*	*chicken (cubed)*
1	*cup*	*uncooked malagkit or plain rice*
1	*small*	*onion (chopped)*
1	*Tbsp*	*garlic (minced)*
1		*ginger root (sliced)*
6	*cups*	*water or broth*
		fish sauce
		virgin coconut oil
		salt to taste
1	*Tbsp*	*scallions (for garnishing)*

1. In a medium sauce pan, sauté garlic, onion, and ginger in oil until onions are translucent.

2. Add chicken and fish sauce and continue cooking on medium heat until lightly browned.

3. Drain any remaining oil and then add rice. Add 2 cups water and bring to boil.

4. Continue cooking, stirring occasionally, until chicken is tender and rice is done (add hot water if necessary).

5. Season with fish sauce according to taste.

Serve hot in a bowl. Garnish on top with fried scallions.

Homemade Pizza Dough

2	*tsp*	*instant yeast*
1	*tsp*	*sugar*
1/3	*cup*	*warm water (110°F/43°C)*
1 1/4	*cup*	*warm water (110°F/43°C)*
2	*tsp*	*honey*
2 1/2	*tsp*	*salt*
2	*Tbsp*	*olive oil*
3 1/2	*cups*	*flour*

1. Dissolve the yeast and sugar in the 1/3 cup warm water. Let it proof until puffy, about 10 minutes.

2. Stir together the yeast mixture, remaining warm water, honey, salt, olive oil and 1 cup of the flour in a large mixing bowl. Whisk until blended. Add remaining flour, a little at a time. Turn out the dough onto a floured board and let rest for 5 to 10 minutes while you wash the bowl and rub it with a few teaspoons of olive oil. Then knead dough for 3 minutes.

3. Place dough in bowl and turn to coat it well with the olive oil. Let rise for about 1 hour, or until doubled in bulk.

4. Punch down dough. At this point you may form the pizzas, or refrigerate the dough for several hours, wrapped tightly in plastic so it won't dry out. (Although a refrigerator rest is not necessary, it makes the dough easier to handle.)

5. After forming crusts, coat top with a little olive oil to prevent sauce from soaking into crust. Then apply sauce.

Makes enough dough for 2 12" pizzas, or 2 10" thick-crust pizzas.

Homemade Pizza

1/2		*onion (small dice)*
1/2		*bell pepper (small dice)*
2	*cloves*	*garlic (minced)*
1	*can*	*tomato sauce*
		oregano, salt, pepper, thyme basil, rosemary to taste

1. Prepare sauce. Place a small amount of olive oil in a saucepan and saute first 3 ingredients until soft. Add tomato sauce and spices and simmer for 10 minutes.

2. Prepare toppings by cutting vegetables, fruit, olives, etc., to desired size. Cook meats until done. Grate cheeses.

3. Assemble by adding sauce to pizza dough (see previous page). Spread until even.

4. Add toppings and cheese.

5. Bake in 450°F (232°C) oven for 10 to 15 minutes or until cheese begins to brown. Serve immediately.

CHAPTER 10

Sauces & Gravies

Sauces and gravies are simple and easy to make. They can save a dry (or overcooked) main dish... or make a good meal even better.

A great sauce can be made in a matter of minutes and will add a delicious moistness to dry or over-cooked meat, poultry or fish. All you need are some drippings, fruit juice or other flavoring. You don't need those ready made mixes. They are expensive and usually have unhealthy or even contraindicated ingredients added. Learning how to make your basic roux for thickening sauces and gravies is essential. The following guidelines make it easy.

Working with a roux to make gravies

A roux is the thickener for many sauces and gravies. The important part to making a roux is to mix an equal volume of fat and flour in a pan. Heat on a low heat for a few minutes while stirring constantly. Then you MUST add cold liquid to the roux and stir constantly until it boils. (If you add hot liquid to the hot roux, you will have lumpy sauce.) Another way to thicken a sauce is to add flour or corn starch to a cold liquid. Mix well until no lumps are present and pour that into your hot liquid, while stirring constantly. This works well for soups, stir fry, and any hot liquid you need to thicken. Make sure the hot liquid is NOT boiling when adding the thickener.

Sauce flavorings

Liquids that are used to make sauces need to be flavorful. Good stocks are a cook's secret ingredient. Instead of water, add a good meat, poultry, veggie or fish stock. The drippings in the bottom of pans used to cook meats or other things can do wonders for your sauce. Add a small amount of water to the pan and scrape with a wooden spoon. Add it to your thickened sauce.

DO NOT SUBSTITUTE MARGARINE FOR BUTTER!

Basic White Sauce
(Béchamel Sauce)

2	*Tbsp*	*virgin coconut oil*
2	*Tbsp*	*onions (chopped)*
2	*Tbsp*	*flour*
2 1/2	*cups*	*milk*
1/2	*tsp*	*salt*
1/4	*tsp*	*white pepper*
1	*pinch*	*nutmeg (grated)*

1. Melt butter in a small, heavy saucepan. As soon as butter is melted, add onions and cook over medium flame for 3 minutes, or until onions begin to turn golden. Stir in flour.

2. Stir in milk and cook, stirring constantly, until smooth. Add salt, pepper, and nutmeg, and cook over low flame for 30 minutes, stirring occasionally. Strain.

3. Makes 2 cups of sauce.

Béchamel (or white) sauce may be prepared in advance, and keeps well in refrigerator for more than 2 weeks.

Note: This sauce is the base for many other sauces. Once you master this you can make just about any thickened sauce. Just vary the liquid and other added ingredients.

Cranberry Sauce

1/4	*cup*	*water*
1/2	*cup*	*orange juice (or 1 can mandarin oranges)*
3/4	*cup*	*sugar*
1/4	*tsp*	*salt*
1	*bag*	*cranberries (12 ounce picked through)*
1/2	*cup*	*chopped pecans (optional)*
2	*Tbsp*	*concentrated pomegranate juice or substitute fresh juice for the water (optional)*

1. Bring water, sugar and salt to a boil in medium, nonreactive saucepan over high heat. Stir occasionally to dissolve sugar.

2. Stir in cranberries and orange juice; return to a boil. Reduce heat to medium; simmer until saucy, slightly thickened, and about two-thirds of berries have popped open. About 5 minutes. Transfer to nonreactive bowl and cool to room temperature.

3. Add optional ingredients and blend well. Note: Can be covered and refrigerated up to 7 days; let stand at room temperature 30 minutes before serving.

This goes well with most meats, poultry and lamb.

Alfredo Sauce

1/2	*cup*	*butter or virgin coconut oil*
1	*cup*	*cream*
1 1/2	*cup*	*parmesan (grated)*
1/2	*tsp*	*salt*
	dash	*white pepper*
		Romano cheese to taste

1. Heat butter and cream in a small saucepan until butter melts. Stir in Parmesan cheese, Romano cheese, salt and pepper. Keep warm over low heat.

Note: For some additional variation, add 1/2 cup feta cheese at the same time as the Romano cheese.

Marinara Sauce

28	*oz*	*can Italian tomatoes (crushed)*
1/4	*cup*	*olive oil or virgin coconut oil*
1/2	*cup*	*red wine or water*
1	*large*	*onion (chopped)*
1	*tsp*	*dried sweet basil*
3	*cloves*	*garlic (minced)*
1/2	*tsp*	*oregano (dried)*
2	*Tbsp*	*tomato paste*
1/2	*cup*	*water*
28	*ozs*	*tomato puree*
		salt and pepper to taste

1. Sauté the onions in the olive oil until lightly browned. Add the garlic and sauté for one minute more.

2. Add all other ingredients and simmer 2 hours, stirring often to prevent sticking.

Note: May add meat, mushrooms, olives, green peppers, spinach, etc., to add variety and make it yours.

Meat or Poultry Gravy

3	*Tbsp*	*fat (butter, olive oil, virgin coconut oil or fat from cooking meat)*
3	*Tbsp*	*flour*
2	*cups*	*stock or water*
		pan drippings
		salt and pepper to taste

1. De-glaze the meat pan with the stock or water. Let cool.

2. Add fat and flour to small saucepan. Cook on low heat for 1 or 2 minutes.

3. Add the cooled stock to the pan, stirring constantly until it boils. Season.

Garlic Tomato Sauce for Veggies

1	*head*	*garlic (peeled)*
		olive oil or virgin coconut oil
6 to 10		*Italian tomatoes (peeled cored, seeded and cut up*
1		*onion (peeled, left whole)*
1/4	*tsp*	*salt*
1	*tsp*	*basil*

1. In a baking dish with a lid, place the onion in the middle. Surround it with the garlic and tomatoes. Sprinkle on the salt and basil. Drizzle all with the olive oil. Make sure you coat the onion well.

2. Cover and bake at 375°F (191°C) for about 1 hour. Checking once to make sure it is not sticking or burning.

3. When it is done, place all in a blender and puree for a few minutes or until thick. Use over cooked broccoli, asparagus, potatoes, or any other veggies you like.

CHAPTER 11

Beverages

Instead of your morning orange juice, why not have a fruit or vegetable smoothie? Your family may not like eating their fruits and vegetables, but most people will "drink" them.

If possible, when making fruit and vegetable drinks, include everything, not just the juice. A trick I use to help make it easier is to cut and clean fruits and veggies ahead of time and freeze them in plastic bags (it's a great way to use bananas that are starting to get a little too ripe). Then you can pick what sounds good and throw it in a blender with some ice and a little liquid. A few seconds later, you have a great beverage. To fancy it up for friends, add a sprig of mint or a bit of fruit for some color.

If your family balks at the pulp in their drink, try removing some of it or add some pulp-less juice to thin the drink. Then, as time goes by, gradually add less juice so they have a chance to get used to a thicker drink. Start out slow, especially with the green juices, and don't use the same combination every day. You can also hide a lot of things in smoothies, such as vitamins supplements, whey protein powder, spinach, or raw eggs (see pasteurization methods on next page). If you add protein powder, make sure it is soy and legume free.

Below is a list of some common fruits and vegetables that are recommended as starters. The foods in red are also known to contain nutrients that help build red blood cells.

apples	celery	lettuce, dark leafy	pineapple
bananas	cranberries	mangos	spinach
beets	cucumbers	oranges	sweet potatoes
berries	grapefruit	papayas	tomatoes
cabbage	grapes	pears, hard	yams
carrots	kale	peppers	watermelons

Pasteurizing Eggs

The overall risk of egg contamination is very, very small. However, if eating raw eggs is a concern for you, you can either purchase pasteurized eggs, or pasteurize them at home. There are several pasteurizing methods available on the internet that you can use. We have included the methods below as they don't require a thermometer, multiple whisks or a double boiler. All pasteurization methods are designed to heat the egg up to at least 140°F (60°C) for just a few seconds, which will kill any harmful bacteria and not cook the egg. The following methods can be adapted to all your recipes that call for raw eggs.

Whole Eggs:

In a heavy saucepan, stir together the eggs and either sugar, water or other liquid from the recipe (at least 1/4 cup of sugar, or liquid, or a combination per egg). Cook over low heat, stirring constantly, until the egg mixture coats a metal spoon with a thin film or reaches 160°F (71°C). Immediately place the saucepan in ice water and stir until the egg mixture is cool. Proceed with the recipes

Egg Yolks:

In a heavy saucepan, stir together the egg yolks and liquid (lemon juice, water, etc.) from the recipe (at least 2 tablespoons liquid per yolk). Cook over very low heat, stirring constantly, until the yolk mixture coats a metal spoon with a thin film, bubbles at the edges or reaches 160°F (71°C). Immediately place the saucepan in ice water and stir until the yolk mixture is cool. Proceed with the recipe.

Egg Whites:

In a heavy saucepan, the top of a double boiler or a metal bowl placed over water in a saucepan, stir together the egg whites and sugar from the recipe (at least 2 tablespoons sugar per white), water (1 teaspoon per white) and cream of tartar (1/8 teaspoon per each 2 whites). Cook over low heat or simmering water, beating constantly with a portable mixer at low speed, until the whites reach 160°F (71°C). Pour into a large bowl. Beat on high speed until the whites stand in soft peaks. Proceed with the recipe.

Note: You must use sugar to keep the whites from coagulating too rapidly. Test with a thermometer as there is no visual clue to doneness. If you use an unlined aluminum saucepan, eliminate the cream of tartar or the two will react and create an unattractive gray meringue.

[1]This information was adapted from: http://whatscookingamerica.net/Eggs/FAQ.htm.

Easy Eggnog

2		*eggs (beaten well)*
3	*tbs*	*sugar, honey or agave*
1	*tsp*	*vanilla*
1/8	*tsp*	*nutmeg (ground)*
2 1/3	*cups*	*milk*

Blend all the ingredients together and serve chilled.

Spiced Hot Apple Cider

1	*qt*	*apple cider (fresh)*
1	*cup*	*sugar*
1/8	*tsp*	*salt*
4		*pieces stick cinnamon*
6		*cloves*
1/4	*tsp*	*allspice*

1. Mix ingredients and bring to the boiling point.
2. Remove from heat and let stand for several hours.
3. When ready to serve remove spices and reheat.

Note: Remove spices sooner for milder version.

Honey Fruit Milk-Shakes

1	*pint*	*frozen yogurt*
OR		
1	*pint*	*vanilla ice cream*
2 1/2	*cups*	*strawberries*
OR		
2 1/2	*cups*	*assorted berries*
1/2	*cup*	*milk*
1/4	*cup*	*honey*
4		*small mint sprigs*

1. Combine all ingredients except mint sprigs in blender or food processor and process about 30 seconds or until smooth.

2. Pour into tall glasses. Garnish with mint sprigs.

Fruit & Vegetable Smoothies

1	cup	fresh squeezed orange juice
2		mangos or equivalent other fruits
8	ozs	frozen fruit
1		banana (fresh or frozen)
2	Tbsp	pomegranate juice concentrate
1	tsp	honey or maple syrup (optional)

1/2		of a red pepper
1	cup	frozen pineapple (paritally thawed)
2-3		mini carrots
1/4	cup	protein powder (find a brand without soy or other additives)
		cilantro to taste

2		red peppers
2		Roma tomatoes
1	stick	celery top, with leaves
2-3		mini carrots
1	slice	lime (thick)
1	pinch	salt (to taste)
		cumin or chili powder (optional, if you like it spicy)

1. Blend all ingredients and serve.

Blueberry Smoothie

Contributed by Samantha Jackson

2	*cups*	*blueberries (frozen)*
1/4		*banana (sliced and frozen)*
1/4	*cup*	*protein powder (find a brand without soy or other additives)*
2	*Tbsp*	*plain yogurt*
1/4	*cup*	*milk or cream*
1	*cup*	*apricot nectar*
		ice cubes (approximately 5 or 6)
2	*Tbsp*	*agave or honey (optional)*

1. Put everything in blender accept agave.
2. Use the pulse setting on the blender until ice cubes and frozen fruits are starting to break up.
3. Turn blender on high until it's the right texture for you.
4. Add agave or honey to taste.

Peach Berry Ice

3		*peaches*
1	*cup*	*milk*
2	*tsp*	*vanilla extract*
1/2	*cup*	*raspberries (or other fruit)*
1	*cup*	*ice (crushed)*

1. Slice the fresh peaches and combine with milk in a blender.

2. Add vanilla and raspberries. Process until smooth. Pour over finely crushed ice.

Fresh Strawberry Lemonade

1 1/2	*cup*	*strawberries (hulled + halved)*
1/4	*cup*	*agave nectar*
2 1/2	*cups*	*fresh water*
		juice of 2 large lemons
		extra strawberries for garnish

1. Blend strawberries, lemon juice and agave on high until quite smooth.

2. Pour into a pitcher and add water. Whisk to combine and refrigerate until well chilled. Serve over ice and garnish each glass with a strawberry.

3. Makes approximately 6, 8 ounce glasses.

Note: Using only 2 lemons gives it that tart lemony flavor without having to add tons of sweetener. To get the most juice out of your lemon, put it in the microwave for 10 seconds before squeezing. If you want it more lemony, add the juice of 2 additional lemons (4 total) and another 1/4 cup of agave (1/2 cup total) to the blender before adding water.

CHAPTER 12

Desserts & Snacks

If they won't eat their fruit, try making it into a dessert.

Fruit desserts, or oatmeal cookies with dried fruit in them, are good and they contribute antioxidants to the diet. They are a much better way to satisfy that sweet tooth than candy.

As a general rule, people with G6PD Deficiency should avoid refined carbohydrates, but they do not have to avoid them entirely. The recipes in this section can be improved by using unrefined sugar, agave, molasses, stevia or some other natural sweetener. Artificial sweeteners should be avoided.

You should watch for artificial food coloring in canned fruit and fruit products. Use fresh or frozen organic fruit whenever possible.

Also, look for added sulfites in dried fruit. We cannot convert sulfites to sulfates which causes many people with G6PDD problems. For further information about sulfur products in drugs and foods, go to the contraindicated page at *g6pddeficiency.org.* Naturally occurring sulfur in onions and garlic, and the sulfur in Epsom salts, are not a problem.

DO NOT SUBSTITUTE MARGARINE FOR BUTTER!

Quick Cobbler

1	*cup*	*flour*
1	*cup*	*sugar (see chapter introduction)*
1	*tsp*	*baking powder*
1/2	*cup*	*milk*
1/2	*cup*	*butter or virgin coconut oil*
2	*cups*	*fruit (fresh, frozen or canned)*

1. Melt butter or coconut oil in 13" x 9" baking pan.

2. Mix flour, sugar, baking powder, and milk together until smooth.

3. Spread mix on top of melted butter. Pour fruit over top.

4. Bake at 375°F (190°C) about 30 minutes or until golden brown.

5. Serve with whipped cream or vanilla ice cream

Apple Oatmeal Cookies

3/4	*cup*	*butter or virgin coconut oil*
1 1/4	*cups*	*brown sugar (firmly packed)*
1		*large egg*
1/4	*cup*	*milk*
1 1/2	*tsp*	*vanilla extract*
1	*cup*	*flour*
1/2	*tsp*	*salt*
1 1/4	*tsps*	*ground cinnamon*
1/4	*tsp*	*baking soda*
1/4	*tsp*	*ground nutmeg*
3	*cups*	*quick-cooking rolled oats*
1		*baking apple (peeled & finely diced)*
3/4	*cup*	*golden raisins*
3/4	*cup*	*chopped nuts (walnuts or pecans)*

1. Preheat oven to 375°F (190°C).

2. In a large bowl, combine butter, brown sugar, egg, milk and vanilla. Beat at medium speed until well blended.

3. In a small bowl, combine flour, salt, cinnamon, baking soda and nutmeg. Gradually add to creamed mixture, mixing just until combined. Using a wooden spoon, stir in oats, apples, raisins and walnuts.

4. Drop rounded tablespoons of dough about 2" apart onto greased cookie sheets. Bake 10 minutes or until just set.

5. Remove from oven and cool about 2 minutes, then transfer to wire racks and cool completely.

Pie Crust

This makes a very flaky pie crust, and you will be sure to get compliments.

3	*cups*	*all-purpose flour (low gluten)*
1 1/2	*tsp*	*salt*
1	*cup*	*virgin coconut oil (maysubstitute a tablespoon of butter for equal amount of virgin coconut oil)*
1/2	*cup*	*cold water*

1. Coconut oil should be solid, but not too stiff. Too warm and it becomes liquid and too cold and it is hard and not easily worked.

2. Put flour and salt into a large bowl and mix well.

3. Spoon the coconut oil into the flour and use a pastry cutter to cut the oil into the flour until it resembles corn meal.

4. Add the water and mix with a spoon until it forms a ball. Over working it at this point will cause your pie crust to be hard. If it won't form a ball, you can add a couple tablespoons of water. It should be a bit dry, but workable.

5. Cover and let rest for a few minutes.

6. Roll to desired shape and thickness.

Fruit Salsa & Cinnamon Chips

2		kiwis (peeled and diced)
2		Golden Delicious apples (peeled, cored and diced)
8	oz	raspberries
1	lb	strawberries
2	Tbsp	white sugar, honey or agave
1	Tbsp	brown sugar
3	Tbsp	fruit preserves (any flavor)
10		flour tortillas (10")
		butter or coconut oil
2	cups	cinnamon sugar

1. In a large bowl, thoroughly mix kiwis, Golden Delicious apples, raspberries, strawberries, white sugar, brown sugar and fruit preserves. Cover and chill in the refrigerator at least 15 minutes.

2. Preheat oven to 350°F (176°C).

3. Coat one side of each flour tortilla with butter or coconut oil. Cut into wedges and arrange in a single layer on a large lightly greased baking sheet. Sprinkle wedges with desired amount of cinnamon sugar.

4. Bake in the preheated oven for 8 to 10 minutes. Repeat with any remaining tortilla wedges. Allow to cool approximately 15 minutes. Serve with chilled fruit mixture.

Strawberry Shortcake

fresh or frozen strawberries

sugar or agave to taste

pie crust (see recipe this chapter)

whipped cream (optional)

1. Make one recipe of pie crust (see recipe in this chapter) for two quarts of strawberries. Roll out, cut into 1" wide strips and place on a cookie sheet to bake.

2. Clean and remove stems from strawberries. Cut into 1/2" pieces and put into a large bowl. Add sugar to taste and mash with a potato masher until mostly mashed but chunks still remain. Let sit in refrigerator while pie crust cooks and cools to room temperature.

3. Crumple pie crust into a serving bowl so that it covers the bottom of the bowl and add strawberries until all pie crust is covered. The exact ratio of strawberries to pie crust will vary depending on taste.

4. Top with whipped cream and serve immediately.

Fruit Pizza

1 1/2	*cups*	*cake flour*
6	*Tbsp*	*butter or virgin coconut oil*
1		*egg*
1	*tsp*	*baking soda*
1/4	*tsp*	*salt*
1	*tsp*	*cream of tarter*
1	*cup*	*sugar (see chapter introduction)*
8	*ozs*	*cream cheese (softened)*
2	*tsps*	*pineapple juice*
3	*cups*	*fruit*

1. Mix together flour, 1/2 cup sugar, butter, egg, baking soda and salt. Press into a 12-inch round, greased pizza pan.

2. Bake 10 minutes at 350°F (176°C). Cool in the refrigerator. Mix cream cheese, remaining sugar and pineapple juice. Spread over cooled crust.

3. Slice fruit into thick slices. Arrange sliced fruit over the crust and filling.

4. Cool thoroughly and cut into eight wedges for serving.

Note: Choose a variety of fruit for this dish. Make it colorful and fun. Good choices include blueberries, strawberries, pineapple, mandarin oranges, kiwi, pitted cherries, bananas, peaches, apples, etc. Be creative and use fruit your family likes. Fresh or frozen organic fruit is best, if available.

Bread Pudding

2	*cups*	*milk*
1/4	*cup*	*butter or virgin coconut oil*
1/2	*cup*	*sugar*
1	*tsp*	*ground cinnamon or nutmeg*
1/4	*tsp*	*salt*
2		*eggs (slightly beaten)*
6	*cups*	*dry multigrain bread cubes*
1/2	*cup*	*raisins or other dried fruit*

1. Heat oven to 350º.

2. Heat milk and margarine in 2-quart saucepan over medium heat until margarine is melted and milk is hot.

3. Mix sugar, cinnamon, salt and eggs in large bowl with wire whisk until well blended. Stir in bread cubes and raisins. Stir in milk mixture.

4. Pour into ungreased 1 1/2 quart casserole or square 8" × 8" × 2" baking dish. Place casserole in 13" × 9" × 2" pan and pour boiling water into the rectangular pan until 1 inch deep.

5. Bake uncovered 40 to 45 minutes or until knife inserted 1 inch from edge of casserole comes out clean.

Almond Butter and Jam Bars

1/2	cup	sugar
1/2	cup	packed brown sugar
1/2	cup	virgin coconut oil
1/2	cup	almond butter
1		egg
1 1/4	cups	all-purpose flour
3/4	tsp	baking soda
1/2	tsp	baking powder
1/2	cup	red raspberry jam

VANILLA DRIZZLE

2	Tbsp	butter or virgin coconut oil
1	cup	powdered sugar
1	tsp	vanilla
3-4	tsps	hot water

1. Heat oven to 350ºF (176°C).

2. Beat sugars, shortening, peanut butter and egg in large bowl with electric mixer on medium speed, or mix with spoon. Stir in flour, baking soda and baking powder.

3. Reserve 1 cup dough. Press remaining dough in ungreased 13" × 9" × 2" pan. Spread with jam. Crumble reserved dough and sprinkle over jam; gently press into jam. Bake 20 to 25 minutes or until golden brown.

4. Cool completely.

5. Drizzle with Vanilla Drizzle.

6. Cut into 8 rows by 4 rows

VANILLA DRIZZLE:

Melt butter in 1 quart saucepan over low heat. Remove from heat and stir in powdered sugar and vanilla. Stir in hot water, 1 teaspoon at a time, until smooth and thin enough to drizzle.

Fruit Flavored Yogurt

Unflavored live culture yogurt

Fruit

Concentrated pomegranate juice

Sweetener to taste

1. Add mashed or finely diced fruit to the yogurt and sweeten to taste. Use agave or stevia.

Notes: You can add some cream and freeze if you like. If the fruit juice is too thin, thicken with some unflavored gelatin. Experiment with different fresh or frozen fruits.

Fruit Kabobs

Fruit (cut into chunks if necessary)

Yogurt (any flavor watch for food color)

Coconut or Chopped nuts

1. Use a variety of fresh fruit that your kids like. Prepare it by washing and cutting into bite sized pieces.

2. Thread onto skewers in an attractive pattern until the skewers are almost full.

3. Roll in yogurt and then into the coconut or nuts.

Note: Use your imagination and make them interesting, attractive and fun.

Index

The foods listed in *red* are known to aid in the production of red blood cells, and/or have high antioxidant properties when served fresh.

D

E

F

N

O

P

Q

R

S

CPSIA information can be obtained
at www.ICGtesting.com
Printed in the USA
FFHW01n0109290918
48581715-52509FF

9 780986 176807